BUCK PETERSON'S COMPLETE GUIDE
TO DEER HUNTING

BUCK PETERSON'S
Complete Guide
to Deer Hunting

by B.R. "Buck" Peterson

Illustrations by J. Angus "Sourdough" McLean

TEN SPEED PRESS

Information contained within this guidebook has been sworn to by very reputable game officials, responsible game biologists, senior park rangers and sober oldtimers as they could be found. But something could still go wrong and Buck assumes no responsibility for anything that does. Ditto Ten Speed Press.

TEN SPEED PRESS
P O Box 7123
Berkeley, California 94707

Cover design by Fifth Street Design

Book design by faith and folly

Illustrations by J. Angus "Sourdough" McLean

Library of Congress Cataloging-in-Publication Data

Peterson, B. R.

    Buck Peterson's complete guide to deer hunting.

    1. Deer hunting—Humor. I. Title. II. Title:
Complete guide to deer hunting.
SK301.P48   1989   799.2'77357   89-4508
ISBN 0-89815-291-7

Printed in the United States of America

14   15   —   96   95

Dedication

Deer hunting was introduced and taught to me by two gentle-men of the northern Minnesota woods. It is to these master hunters, my uncle and his late hunting buddy, who have seasoned my life with hunting health and humor, that this irreverent guide book is dedicated.

Contents

Introduction

Not long ago while Buck was hot on the trail of another record-busting deer in its prime Minnesota habitat, he was struck by the thought that once he goes to the big hunting camp in the sky, a large gut pile of hunting wisdom may be lost to future generations forever. That certainly would be a fine kettle of camp meats!

Why, oh why does Buck hunt deer? Is it for some swarmy reunion with Mother Nature and all her splendors, a soft-focus communion with primal instincts? Nope!

It's because Buck likes the taste of venison! He likes it fried, broiled, pickled and jerkied. He likes it for breakfast, brunch, lunch, high tea, early supper and late night dinner. If he's got lots, he may share. If he's got just a little, it'll be hoarded and the closest you'll get to his pan fry is the smell leaking out under his back door. He likes it raw, red, pink, burned to a crisp. He likes it on a plate, in his hands, on the floor. It can be sliced and diced, cubed and coddled, flaked and baked. He likes to chew it into little pieces and adding a few carrots, makes a fine "mouth stew." He'll gulp large chunks, forcing gag reflexes that bring it up again for another chew! He'll throw a chop in a cuisinart for a real Bloody Mary. He'll try to eat it slow but always rushes to the last bite, which he'll let lay in the back of his mouth, feeling the muscle molecules break down in his digestive juices. He'll eat the heart, the liver, the cheeks, the lips, all but the feathers. Buck is not a happy hunter without venison.

Buck Peterson's *Complete Guide to Deer Hunting* was written for all deer hunters, young and old, and starts where the other deer hunting books leave off. The "Guide" (as it's popularly called) is not just another magazine article thinly stretched over the bones of a book! In fact, this is the last book you'll need on deer hunting and it should have been your first! Give all the other books away. There are secrets in the "Guide" that many famous outdoor writers have tried to learn by following Buck on his trips. Several of the younger, lazier ones have even offered Buck's friends money and excess sporting goods for a few tips and a good map of his hunting grounds.

The Guide is a working document to follow you everywhere and designed to be put in the glovebox of your 4X4. It won't guarantee a Boone and Crockett trophy. It won't even help you shoot a deer. Your odds of seeing one—especially in Wisconsin—are much too slim for that. It is intended to help you get along and to take care of business. This book includes items of protocol and etiquette; it's a Mr. Manners of the woods. It tells you how to be a good guy, a good hunting buddy and a true and decent sportsman. It's a little thinner than most guidebooks because Buck doesn't accept any advertising and didn't include grainy black and white photos of the carnage from his camp. It is, however, just chuckful of suggestions, tips and anecdotes and if this book doesn't help you bag a Bambi, maybe one of your more successful hunting partners will share some with you. It is also a required textbook in Buck Peterson's Wilderness School and Famous Sportsman Correspondence Course and is another volume in Buck's paperbound treasury of Guides to Hunting Skills, Manliness and Outdoor Happiness.

The Ten Most Frequently Asked Questions About Deer And Deer Hunting

1. *Do deer mate for life, like geese and people who read good books?*
No. Bucks have the morals of a billy goat, always flirting with the new girls. Does, if they had their druthers (which they don't), would prefer to live a monogamous lifestyle.

2. *Do deer really feel like deer, you know, or are they just like people in deer clothing?*
Only deer that are well-traveled question their "deer-ness." These heightened sensibilities, often found in animals of questionable gender, are very dangerous to a deer's survival during hunting season.

3. *Should I hunt early in the season?*
Yes, deer are more trusting and can even be petted then. Some crusty oldtimers say the spooked animal full of adrenaline tastes better. Hunt these critters the last day.

4. *Do deer wipe after going #2?*
Yes, but only in northern climates. Their southern cousins show less concern with personal hygiene. Northern deer wipe by scooting along the ground on their butt like a dog that has swallowed a string.

5. *Can deer catch AIDS from the use of dirty pine needles?*
There is no conclusive evidence either way.

6. *Is the woods just like the books say—fluffy snow, bright colored leaves, crystal-clear reflective ponds, full of soft cuddly animals with names like Mr. Owl?*
In Buck's neck of the woods, yes!

7. *How can you tell a buck's age?*
The antlers start sagging first. Then instead of only thinking about the next doe, the older ones concentrate on finding and enjoying a good meal. The real old ones just pray for a painless bowel movement.

8. *What do deer hunting guides do once the non-resident dudes go to bed?*

Contrary to popular belief, they are not getting "gear" ready for tomorrow. They are sitting around the campfire, talking and laughing about the bozo hunters in tents 1 & 2.

9. *Do deer like being deer?*

Modern stresses and strains are producing increasing numbers of urban deer that would rather be another large animal like a moose or elk. There is no evidence of deer wanting to be a smaller animal, like a squirrel.

10. *Where did the phrase "buck naked" come from?*

It refers to a rare public sighting of Buck bathing in a high mountain stream and it was soon after that the term "trophy racks" popped into our language!

THE HUNTED

The Different Kinds

MULE DEER: In Latin, they are called *odocoileus hemionus*, meaning half ass or mule. This is misleading as their hind quarters are very complete and not to be tampered with. It's believed that the term refers to the game official that hung that name on them.

Mule deer have thick necks, are easier to hunt than whitetail, and can be fooled by most methods of hunting. They are mostly found in the West, in mountain retreats, but sometimes in open country. Mule deer are built like Polish women—stocky bodies with thick legs and big, ugly feet.

Mulies have large, mule-like ears for listening across mountain passes and a thin tail with black tip which is left down due to an overriding concern with public decency. Mule deer have the heaviest antlers and are the largest animals in the deer world.

In British Columbia, mule deer are called a subspecies of black-tailed deer but once again, the hockey pucks have it all *hemionus*-backwards.

WHITETAILED DEER: Lewis and Clark, a couple of lost souls from St. Louis, first saw and described this animal as "common deer." They are more properly descendants of "Virginia's Deer." It's not too clear in the history books who this Virginia was but it's thought she was a plantation owner's wife who dabbled, without her husband's knowledge, in animal husbandry.

Whitetailed deer are found most everywhere in North America but prefer the eastern climates. They are found in abundance near Buck's stand.

These animals are a little smaller, more delicate and certainly more skittish than their western cousins. They have blacker noses and a white tail and rump. They are slender, dainty, high-strung prima donnas with neuroses only dreamt about by fauna-Freuds. They like to stay close to home, much like their smaller, slower woodland friends. Their tail movements are different than mule deer; when flat or slightly twitching, all is ok. If sticking straight out—warning; and if up and waving, that wave is for you.

2

Subspecies such as Coues deer in New Mexico and Arizona are the preferred sport for short people, as these dwarf-like animals with big racks look good hanging in their little houses.

OUT OF SEASON DEER: These animals, a mix of the above, are easier to shoot but more difficult to get home. They are best identified with hand-held spotlights. If a warden comes up on you after you've accidentally shot and started to gut one of these deer, look outraged, pinch the deer's nose shut and start mouth to mouth resuscitation immediately, pushing firmly on the rib cage.

OUT OF RANGE DEER: This animal is a favorite of non-resident hunters and pursued with a whole volley of shots, swinging wide vertically or horizontally, spraying the bullets in an arc that the critter can't avoid. Fully automatic weapons are used in this complicated type of shoot. God, Mother Nature, and Jimmy the Greek co-operating, you'll connect. The junior members of the camp will bring these animals out.

CAMP DEER: These animals are the best tasting and are provided by states that have an active concern for happy, well-fed hunters who will continue to buy over-priced non-resident licenses. Some states say you have to make all killed game part of your daily bag limit - it's not too clear exactly what that means.

The Different Sexes

MALE: Male deer, or bucks, are the ceremonial head of the deer household and the major breadwinner. They have two key distinguishing features:

The Antler: Antlers are a rack of calcified bone, which, unlike horns, are shed every year. When this head of "horn" is growing, calcium is pulled, often violently and without just cause, from other parts of their body and must be replenished by an extraordinary quantity of acorns, small rodents, and stuffed wild mushrooms. In the battle for calcium share, the hips will usually win causing the antlers to lose their stiffness and fall loose on the head, flopping like old spaghetti when the buck runs.

Mule Deer Antlers
Single Forks

Whitetail Antlers
Multiple Forks

Game wardens and nature walkabouts have come upon deer, admittedly on rare occasion, in which the calcium had been pulled up so abruptly that the leg bones had collapsed, but the deer sure had a good-looking magnum rack. The rack is an object of veneration by other smaller bucks and by all does. It is the current yardstick to determine trophy animals.

Antler growth begins with the deer's pineal gland telling the brain to push some velvet-encased blood vessels up in the air. A little later, the cajones stew up a nice batch of male hormones to tighten them up and then stop their growth, cutting off the blood supply. The antlers are now hard and the velvet gets rubbed off as it dries. The act of rubbing is an erotic act for trophy hunters.

Occasionally a doe without enough female hormones to block antler growth can end up with male headgear and these unfortunate creatures are called lesbucks by respected game biologists. A change of diet, weekly shots, and herd counseling can be considered only temporary treatments of this difficult condition.

After the hunting season, all antlers fall off as the animal walks downhill, leaving big, ugly bald spots. If all the bucks in a herd grow their antlers at the same time, they'll shed them at the same time too, setting off such a clatter that does lying in their beds will jump up to see what's the matter. The big bucks will feel extremely lightheaded for a while. A difficult shedding produces severe migraine headaches and is just another cross a mature animal must bear.

The size of the antlers is determined by how good the groceries are in the neighborhood, the buck's genes, and the general living conditions of the animal. A very young buck, given the right circumstances, can have a monster rack in the first season and these child prodigies are very precocious.

The Schwantz: The buck's male organ, or "el grande," once removed from a truly dead animal, is a valuable memento of a good hunt. In many Third World countries and in certain neighborhoods in Los Angeles, "los bones" have religious significance and are displayed in shrines with loud, fast, but danceable music. In the loving hands of a craftsman, it can be made into a neat little coin purse and a great gift for the little lady. Remember, the hunting season is immediately followed by Christmas.

Other distinguishing features include:

Color: Usually a little darker, especially along the lower cheeks and above the upper lip, producing a shadow late in the day, around 5:00 PM.

Hair density: Thick and matted, except in older bucks where hair starts to thin out on top, starting with a small bald spot and spreading in ever-widening circles.

Speed: Similar to does but, due to lower appendages, must build up a better head of steam to clear barbed wire fences.

Habits: Excessive male bonding and promiscuity in early years; maturing to a protective and covetous collection of a large harem.

Habitat: The core areas for a whitetail buck can go up to 40-50 acres, as they are usually loners. Mule deer bucks are more social and are seen hanging around other four-legged large animals and four-wheeled vehicles.

FEMALE: Female deer, or does, are the more passive and submissive sex. In many states, they are even reduced to be called "antlerless deer." Under pressure from women's groups, state officials in the more liberal northeastern states are lobbying to rename "bucks only" seasons to "titless deer only!"

Does differ from bucks in their ability to reproduce, and exhibit better social skills. Except for certain times of the month, they seem more even-tempered than the males. As in large Italian families, a mature doe is the real head of the household, regardless of what the buck says.

Instead of having just two jugs, female deer have a whole flock of nipples along their belly that are reserved only for the feeding of their young. They can not be used for erotic foreplay. They are sort of just there, much like those of the boss' secretary.

The female organs are where you'd expect them, just south of the beltline, in a spot called the "Great White North." They are as organized and as complicated as a human's and are considered to be major adult deer playthings.

The female deer has a reproductive cycle that a buck enjoys pedalling and comes into heat like an eighteen-year-old cheerleader. The gestation period is marked by increasing irritability, swollen hooves and a higher pitched, almost whiny bleat.

FREE-MALE: There is a third deer sex, called free-males. Once rare, this variety of both mule and white-tailed deer is on the increase, particularly in Northern California and metro New York City. These "beasts-in-transition" are now showing up in larger numbers in game reports and in traditionally "bucks only" areas. The unfortunate creatures of undetermined sex have confused hunters and are described by respected game biologists as female deer in buck's clothing.

The most frequently observed social abnormality is "buck butting." Unlike two typical bucks clashing antlers over a harem, two free-males will BACK into each other, producing noticeable muffled sounds that drive normal deer families to other habitats.

Other differences include a blatant disregard for other deer customs. Free-males are frequent visitors to the "homes" of prosperous does where they spend endless hours talking about the most frivolous things. These deer are somewhat sweeter tasting too. The phrase "pass the buck" originally referred to a price on an animal hide but is now used to describe one of the free-male's little games.

Endangered Species

Federal and state laws protect animals that can't protect themselves and these legislative safety nets prohibit the harvest of the helpless by the traditional methods of hunting. Removed from the day-to-day pressure of a hunting season, the protected animals are free to do whatever they want, even non-deer things. The three principal groupings are:

COLUMBIAN WHITETAIL: Unable to handle the stress of agricultural expansion, these flighty animals are now found only in the Columbia River estuary near Cathlamet, Washington and near Roseburg, Oregon. They are fish eaters and not good eating anyway.

KEY DEER: Originally imported to the Florida Keys by well-meaning Europeans running the drug operations, the dog-sized Key deer were popular pets of large estate owners. Overbreeding pushed their numbers into wilds owned by developers and soon tour companies were formed to thin out their ranks. Wealthy Jewish people and conch store owners in Key West wanted their lively lawn ornaments returned to the old park-like setting and pushed hunting restrictions through a corrupt legislative process. They have initiated a Safe Neighborhood program in the Keys where threatened Key deer can safely hide in the back yards of homes with the familiar up-turned-hand-with-a-deer-hiding-behind-it sign posted on their front lawn. With backstraps the size of a half dollar, these animals are too small to eat anyway and the meat is tainted by their affection for Key Lime pie.

TROPHY BUCKS IN WISCONSIN: Due to the extremely short supply of qualified resident trophy hunters, Wisconsin game officials are considering the importing of "hired guns" to cull the herds. The sharpshooters would be issued complimentary licenses by means of a direct mail campaign to the membership list of the Disabled and Blind Hunters Association of Minnesota. The overpopulation of trophy animals makes for an anxious woods as the stress of carrying both heavy social burdens and heavy antlers can cause the breakdown of the basic family unit.

Deer Signs

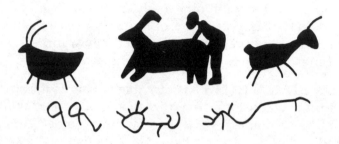

EARLY SIGNS: In caves all over the country, early deer hunters carved their exploits on limestone walls.

The above sample, found by respected game biologists, shows early hunters climbing on their horses to go hunting, proving that you are carrying on traditions of long ago.

MODERN SIGNS AND HOW TO READ THEM: If the sign shows running or leaping deer, that's the only kind they have in that area. If the animals are shown standing still, that's what they'll do for you as you take aim. If there are antlers on the deer, it's a bucks only area and if there are a lot of deer signs around, that means there are a lot of deer around. In parts of Wisconsin, these road signs are provided by the state for pre-season target practice.

Some signs just say what they mean!

THE BUCK
STOPS HERE

Another deer sign is the presence of tire skid marks and big clumps of hair along the roadside. A fresh gut pile is a dead giveaway!

A sure sign of deer:

NO HUNTING   NO TRESPASSING

NATURAL SIGNS
Tracks: Deer have hoofprints that are easy to follow and look like this:

You can also easily tell the difference between does and bucks. Buck tracks are heel-heavy, more authoritative. Doe tracks are light and flighty.

9

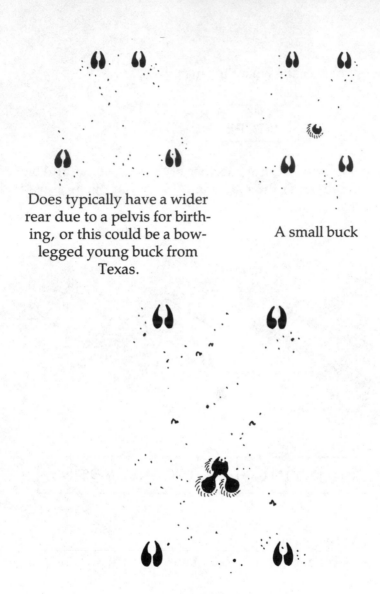

Does typically have a wider rear due to a pelvis for birthing, or this could be a bow-legged young buck from Texas.

A small buck

A real big buck!

Tracks are indications of the activity of the moment. Buck has tracked deer through California cannabis, easily catching up with doped deer giggling through the brush. Young deer will drag their feet on the way to a deer event with their folks. Standing deer may have one extra-deep track if they are counting hunters entering the woods.

More unusual tracks include:

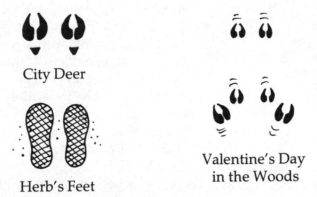

City Deer

Herb's Feet

Valentine's Day
in the Woods

Track Patterns: You'll find track trails and these highways usually connect all the stops in prime deer habitat: water, food, cover, and protection. You'll want to know where deer drink, eat, sleep, and make whoopie!

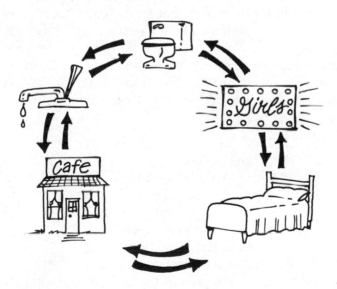

Follow tracks that go both directions otherwise you'll get dizzy. Most deer live in a fixed area so if you do this right, you'll never get lost.

11

Droppings: Deer "scat" are important signs of activity. If the poop pellets are in a thin trail spread over a long grunt, the deer was going Big Job on the run and there is no reason to think he'll slow down even to wipe.

If the marbles are widely scattered, the deer has been scared "scatless" and had an emergency evacuation of the bowels, caused by a true case of Buck (hunter of legend) fever.

If the droppings are stacked in a very neat, precisely arranged pile, you've come upon the embarrassing remains of a free-male deer.

If the droppings are large, black and tarry, with pieces of Fritos, Beer Nuts and an occasional beer bottle cap, your neighbor Herb is in the area.

If you see no scat and know the area has large deer, trophy bucks are holding their poop until they reach deep cover.

Bear and deer scat look a lot alike. It's helpful to know the difference.

Some of the more heroic hunters say they can tell the difference between buck and doe scat. Bull! Buck's good hunting buddy, B. S. (Big Scat) White, says doe scat tastes just a little sweeter.

DEER SCENTS: Much like you, deer have places on their bodies that don't smell good.

For example, they have glands between their toes called interdigitals that produce a sticky, yellow toe-jam that stinks just like your little brother's. These glands are present on all four feet and when the deer is walking around without protective footgear, enough of this gee-gaw goes in the track for another deer to follow. Does can find frisky fawns, and bucks their dreamboats just by following this yellow-thick road. Like most Eastern Europeans and people from Milwaukee, bucks find strong foot odor on their "gals" sexy.

Deer have their armpits down the outside of their hind legs. There are two glands here on each leg; one called the metatarsal, located low on the outside and bordered by soft hair. Not much is known about these except some think fright triggers secretions. The more active tarsals are found inside each hind leg and are surrounded by tufted long hairs. These hairs stand up like hackles when the animal is scared or mad. Deer will urinate on these little powder puffs and, once mixed with the glands' musk, the combined odor is used by bucks to moisten a scrape and as a all-occasion cologne. When an animal is spooked, these tarsals will shoot out a stink that'll empty a woods.

The other important gland is the pre-orbital—a small, little-understood gland in the eye that secretes another signature odor and is passed on leaves during a rub, or maybe it's just sleep gunk that the animals would rub off if they could get their paws up that high. When deer are not crying over their fate as a doomed forest animal, this is the gland that keeps their eyes moist.

Scrapes: During the rut, bucks leave personalized notes all throughout the woods, scraping small areas clear of twigs and leaves, and then leaving his scent for a doe in heat to enjoy.

Scrapes let the does know where the "big guy" will be. These little pee "post-its" are usually six to twenty inches across; they are little, oval dirt depressions, in an area where the buck feels most manly. The active breeding scrapes get up to seven feet in diameter and drive the ladies crazy.

If you see several scrapes within a single area in good cover, you are in a Bambi brothel and should stand close enough to catch all the illicit action. Attracted by a good scrape, does will come by, take a number, and sit in a big buck's "waiting room."

Doe scrapes are increasing in number. Like most Lutheran women, does are embarrassed by their bottoms and by what happens "down there." The prudish does cover their droppings by kick-scraping a dirt cover.

Bucks will scrape a line around their core area. Since whitetails live in a square mile or so, it takes a full summer of busy scraping to make the circle, especially with pesky young bucks messing up the lines. Mule deer find this task almost impossible.

The Rub: Bucks like to rub trees and branches with their headgear for three reasons:

To establish a territory.

To rub old velvet from the new antlers.

To rearrange head lice.

Does enjoy a quick rub on the "D" spot, an erogenous zone right below the tail.

Fawns rub short bushes to get rid of their spots.

If you see rubs, it's most likely a buck is in the neighborhood. Good rubs are bright and shiny from regular use. Dull rubs are from dull deer you don't want to shoot anyway.

During preseason, check for rubs in conjunction with beds and droppings. Several rubs in a row are called a rub line and if you tie a string between each, you'll learn the little world deer live in.

In late season, bucks will still rub but most often on the run which may cause a big buck to get hung up in the branches of low trees, inflicting severe whiplash or even hanging them right on the spot.

In an area with a lot of bucks, there is considerable one-upsmanship—competing bucks rubbing higher and higher than the previous headgear—like hands on a baseball bat. If you see just two footprints next to a tree and a very high rub, a very aggressive buck is nearby.

Veteran deer will rub on the opposite side of the trees in the direction they are heading. Big old bucks will rub small trees to throw a Wisconsin trophy hunter off.

Where Deer Live

IN THE MOUNTAINS:

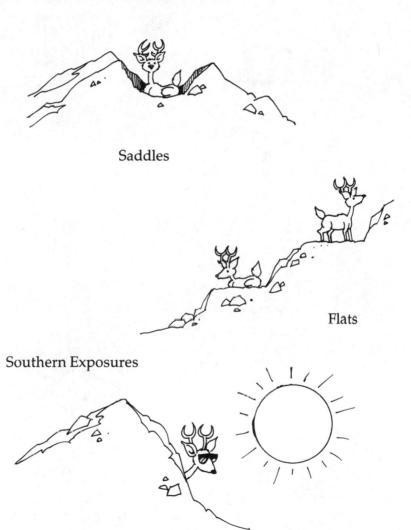

Saddles

Flats

Southern Exposures

ELSEWHERE:

On the Edges of Habitat

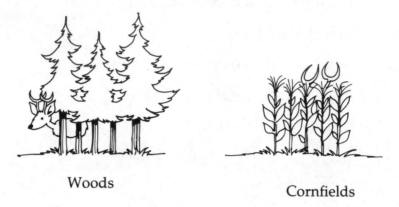

Woods   Cornfields

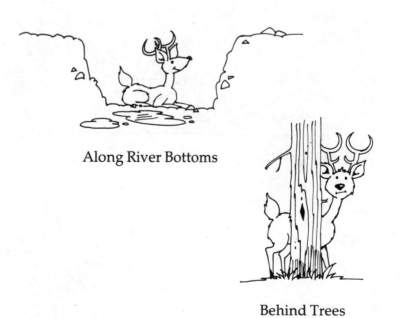

Along River Bottoms

Behind Trees

How They Travel

Deer traditionally move in groups and all share similar configurations:

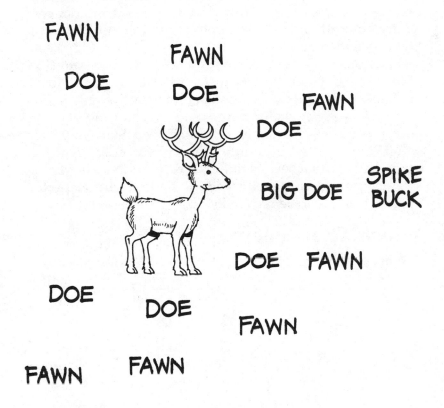

The group will always be formed into a V, patterned after their flying feathered friends. During the hunting season, the inner V will be centered with the Big Buck as shown above. The fawns are too young to be really aware of their role in the formation.

Migrations And Reasons

CHANGE OF FOODS: When winter hits with high snows that cover the groceries, deer will move to lower elevations for a full meal deal.

CHANGE OF SEASONINGS: When the road crews put too much salt on their roadside snacks, deer will move away from the asphalt highways to country dirt roads.

CHANGE OF WEATHER: Less known is the movement of midwestern deer that just don't want to spend another cold winter up north. It's only the ones who can't afford the trip that are condemned to starve in the deeryards of Minnesota and Wisconsin. Just before the first big storm, these travelers group along the state borders, just north of Chicago and south of Minneapolis, and follow the major interstates south, taking care to avoid all population centers and traveling only at night. On rare occasions, truck drivers have spotted them when they aren't all able to squeeze into the road culverts. The exact routes have not yet been verified but with evidence of Minnesota deer found in Missouri and Mississippi, the suspected migration is sure to be proven by closer studies.

Where They Sleep

What you think their beds look like:

What they really look like:

Depending on the size of animal, deer beds are six to eight feet long, dug down into a hollow and surrounded by their favorite things—twigs, berries, leaves and left-behind hunter apparel. Since most does have twin fawns, you'll see many twin-size beds and they graduate to larger beds as necessary—beds having a double role as sleep and frolic area. The King of the herd has his own size bed, the Queen hers. If they have been together for a long time, it's common to see these beds move further apart. Early in a courtship, one bed will be left cold overnight. California deer, while not any larger than others, tend to have longer beds, due to what some biologists describe as a need for "more space."

When deer lie down, does and spike bucks will lay flat, changing sides nightly so one side will not become flatter than another. Pregnant does will find sleeping uncomfortable in any position and will sleep on their backs, with their legs straight up, slightly folded at the knee. Big bucks normally have a much more difficult time sleeping, with their big rack of antlers. A buck's bed will have a hollow at one end where his rack can rest. Restless bucks will sleep like horses, leaning against a tree, particularly if they have been out all night. What some sport hunters do is shoot away the tree and let the fall take its toll. Some deer will sleep with just their head up, eyes closed. Others will sleep with their eyes open but that's really hard on the surface of their eyes and you can identify these deer by how often they have to blink!

Young deer will sleep the night through and play all day. Older deer will try to snooze in the day and do their deer duties at night when hunters are drunk in their sleeping bags. It's not known if deer dream but old timers have heard deer snore, especially the big bucks who have just finished a large meal of nuts and twigs.

Deer sleep where they feel safe but as deer communities are compressed by the scorched earth policies of developers and National Park rangers, game biologists have identified two typical patterns of bedding:

A Crowded Urban Community

Game biologists discover entire families living on just one side of the main trail. The family beds are the sites of all the animal reunions. The more troublesome bucks are found in the early evenings at the major trail junctions, often up to no good.

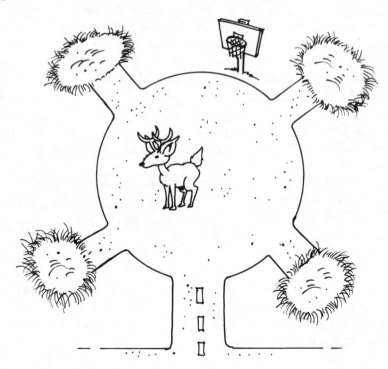

A Crowded Suburban Community

The deer "burbs" are separated from the more concentrated populations by a river, lake, or railroad tracks. The dominant animals live here, with more pronounced social habits and guest quarters. The beds with water frontage are most prized. The best-looking does will mate with the bucks from these neighborhoods. It should be noted that these females are less faithful, and will slip along a back trail between the legs of a bachelor buck should her resident male be away for an extended period of time. Bucks bed with the wind to their backs, facing the driveway. The back yard is never trimmed the way it should be and always faces deep cover. Beds on hillsides rank second in popularity, especially with a view of doe areas or hunting camps.

Eating Habits

It's very important to learn the habits of your quarry, and no habit is more regular than a deer grubbing about for food. If you've done your homework, you'll recognize the half-digested foods inside your critter's gut pile. There are three distinct types of foodstuffs; what they prefer to eat, what their parents taught them to eat, and what will keep them alive.

WHAT THEY EAT: In the woods, deer will browse on leaves, buds, and soft twigs in the spring. A preferred food is the wild mushroom cap stuffed with wild berries. When the leaves turn color, deer reach for elm, cedar, white pine and dogwood twigs, and bend over for sassafras and poison ivy. A favorite is acorns which are also high on the ground squirrel's list and in hard times, oldtimers have reported Boone and Crockett heads chasing ground squirrels for a large nut.

On the flatlands, young, wild grasses and cash crops like wheat and cannabis are staple items in a deer's diet. Fruit and peanuts are an animal's fast food. Deer love sweet corn; holding it between both front feet they eat it as they've been taught, across the row, end to end. In Carter country, deer eat goobers, with the accompanying bad breath. Whitetails will eat all vegetables but have difficulty persuading the fawns to finish their brussels sprouts.

On the mountains, mulies prefer a diet of bitterbrush, rabbit brush, mountain mahogany, ceanothus, and cannabis.

Urban deer gorge on the decorative shrubs found around large condo projects, but this very rich diet must be combined with other, more nutritious grains.

WHEN THEY EAT: Deer prefer to eat at night when they aren't in the crosshairs of some bushwacker. The problem is that they can't see what they are eating, so a stalker will notice a lot of spit-up food from night feeders. If the animals must eat during the more dangerous day, they do so on their knees which is very uncomfortable or lying down which makes it difficult to swallow.

HOW THEY EAT: Except for the two upper front teeth, they have to gum their food. Deer nibble like a suburban housewife at a food fair. Under pressure, they will gulp their food and move on. Deer need roughage and will eat the hard grains just because they feel it's good for them.

WHERE THEY EAT: You can tell where the deer are browsing by noticing the feeding lines on trees:

Fawns have the most difficult time getting above the browse line and must stand on top of each other to have dinner.

Toilet Habits

Deer have to go toilet more often than humans, especially #1.

Bucks will go not only to relieve bladder pressure but to mark their territory, much like a bass fisherman during a backyard beer-b-q. They will urinate standing up in their own scrapes, in other, less dominant deer's scrapes, and on other, smaller sleeping bucks.

Does like to pee together and will do so ten to fifteen times a day. Large groups of does will potty together. The doe potty areas are near water where, once they've done their duty, the does will go gaze into the water at length before heading back to the harem. It should be noted that doe potty areas are much messier than buck biffies and much easier to find. It's almost as if the does don't care about the cleanliness of these areas.

Does squat like a dog, the more experienced raising their tail before going. There are no reports of co-ed toileting but oldtimers have spotted young bucks lurking around doe toilets, hoping to catch a peek of a lifted tail. This behavior really irritates the matriarchs yet the younger does seem flattered by the attention.

All deer must go Big Job, or #2, on a regular basis or experience gastric distress. Their diet, no matter where they live, must be properly balanced with roughage, water, and a sweet now and then for regularity. Deer scat, or poop, is an important indicator of general living activity and full of clues for successful hunting. If the scat is cold and hard, the deer sign is old; if the scat is warm and moist, the deer might be around the next bend so be ready. If the little pellets are hot with just a little crust, be careful as you raise your head. Pellets are oval shaped so the back door doesn't slam shut each time and come in all designer colors from taupe to light camel. To find out what your prized buck is eating, break open a pellet for samples. Crack open with your fingers or if difficult, with your storebought dentures. You may see seeds, twigs and Fritos in each pellet.

Animal Sex

Sex as practiced by large animals has been a lively subject of study by a sub-species of biologists. These sex specialists have spent countless sleepless nights watching deer "doing the deed" and come to exhibit animal-like behavior in their own boudoir.

The deer's favored position is dog-style. During the act, a buck will bark like a dog, changing to a howl towards the end. A large buck will reach up and put his feet over the doe's eyes, adding a little mystery to what, in an established relationship, could become stale sex.

Is there truly safe sex among deer? Yes, if done according to conservative recommendations. Frequently there is the innocent passing of mites or body crabs, but there seems to be no social stigma attached to such a discovery. Only in established herds are there any evidence of deviant sex, and then only among those deer that hang around drive-in movies and shopping malls.

Big bucks prefer to "amour" at night so hunters can't see and interrupt. If a small doe is involved, it's not a pretty sight anyway. If a buck is caught in a "nooner," pull the scope cover down and shoot the buck only if he fails to show post-coital affections.

Like most Catholic women, deer do not practice any effective birth control and their reckless disregard has resulted in the deer population explosion and subsequent expanded seasons and game limits! It's their own fault.

THE RUT: In late summer or early fall when the lights begin to dim, bucks enter a period of their life called the rut. Life in the rut is a time of single-focus activity, a lot like a sailor on shore leave. The male fluids start collecting forward, building pressure from the groin forward ending with a swollen neck. In severe cases, the essential juices will push up into the head, whiting out the normally dark eyes. During this time a buck becomes a four-legged love muscle, raping and pillaging like a Norseman. This condition comes with a pubescent odor, a sweet smell normally associated with Catholic boy's schools.

Bucks will normally "service" six to ten does apiece. The big bucks get all the does. The younguns have to wait until they are three to four years old, roughly middle age in human years before they can have their first taste of honey. The more impatient youngsters in Texas will pop south across the border to break in what's called their "jallopenis!"

The does are normally very receptive while in heat, or estrus. This honeymoon period lasts about 24-36 hours every twenty-eight days between October and December, and some does can have up to three heats in a single season. While she is in heat, a doe will seem to shy away from bucks, hiding her bush behind a bush, even sitting on her powder puff—at the same time flirting, searching for the best buck in the village.

A buck will sniff doe "buffs" on regular rounds and, if one is in heat, the buck will try to lie down with the doe, nuzzling a bit, and making deer promises to have and to hold. Some bucks may bring presents of chewed up acorns. The doe, at this point, will be overcome with emotion. Then they "do it." Once it's all over, the buck will leave to talk over the latest conquest with the other bucks. The done doe will not be receptive to any junior bucks looking for seconds.

After the rut, the most active bucks lose weight, become scraggly looking and get ready to lose their antlers, leaving them truly boneless.

MATING: Read the story of Bambi real close and you'll glean the disgusting fact that Bambi not only married his first cousin, Faline, but even did the "rut" and had children too! Similar to sad tales of the old British monarchy and the incestuous relationships that produced extra long backbones on idiots, this family inbreeding is what first produced tails on deer and is considered by the herd's religious leaders as evidence of original sin. Look close on all the pictures of Noah's Ark and you'll see just tail stubs. There are certain parts of the country, like in the back hills of North Carolina and Georgia, where this sort of thing has been going on for a long time; local oldtimers report that those deer with elongated tails, especially the older bucks, have a hard time getting it up! They have been seen to step on that thick appendage when walking backwards and fall down, to the catcalls of other woodland friends. The tails naturally erase tracks making these trophies very difficult to hunt.

Does choose mates that are winners. They will look for a young buck on the move, preferably from a good family, with good health and skin, a pitch-black nose, and strong lower back teeth. Some does select the sleeker males, with more well-defined musculature and smaller butts. Other does prefer the mature animal knowing that their personalities are more evenly balanced and they don't spend all the daylight hours preening on trail corners. Other does opt for the safety of the harems of trophy bucks and are thought to be the more submissive of the females. In the genetic lorebook that's passed down from generation to generation, these does are usually offshoots from a transcontinental migration of both mixed whitetail and mule deer that left the woodlands of the Midwest under some yet-unexplained habitat stress and are the core nucleus of the large harems found in Utah.

Scientific studies have recently isolated four new mating behavior patterns.

Older buck/preemie doe: These Lolitas of the woods loiter near the stage doors of the stag areas, squealing like groupies, bleating for a little eye contact. A buck in midlife crisis may take a youngun under its "horn;" the herd social leaders publicly disapprove but privately yearn for this activity.

Young buck/older doe: Led astray by an older but still attractive female, the young buck is quickly taught the mysteries of the woods. A wise doe knows how to rub a buck the right way.

Crossing the species line: Generally speaking, whitetailed deer will not mate with mule deer. They consider their western cousins coarse and brutish. When the herds rub together, there is little or no flirting and only pimply faced rebels will cross the "line."

Buck/cow: Only when a buck is overdosed on hormones will he hump a Holstein. Young bucks wouldn't be caught dead with a bossy. On rare occasion, a "longhorn" will teach a whitetail doe a few rough lessons in animal sex.

HAVING CHILDREN: Like farm girls, deer breed in the fall and birth in the spring. The gestation period is about six months long and the actual birth of a fawn is greeted by all the creatures of the forest.

A healthy, well-fed doe will have at least one if not two fawns at a time. There have been rare but increasingly more frequent occurrences of multiple births which are associated with the consumption of high-tech, fast-growing "super" grasses. Deer having quints stay dazed for a full year and seem to lose interest in sex. The doe is finally able to stand up after 6 months. She will seem to carry a grudge against the buck who put her in that "condition" and will shy away from the deer social events that led her to trouble in the first place.

The birthing is in May or June and a fawn will weigh about four pounds. On quiet moonlit nights, you can hear the screams of first-time mothers having oversized animals. The buck will never be around to help when needed. Friends of the doe will attend to all the needs of the new mother.

The little fawns will keep their spots and long lashes until September and will breastfeed until the bucks push them out during the rut. Fawns will stay with the does as long as they can but will grow up without a strong male role model. This can lead to identity problems for the younger bucks.

Growing Up In A Troubled World

The fawn's first shock is the forced landing on the forest floor. The second slap is the reality of a demanding deer world, and deer daycare centers are organized to help busy adult deer raise their offspring. From the first days in these remote centers, fawns learn how to lift their tails, twitch their ears, keep their eyes moist, and chew with their mouths closed.

Most experts say deer stay in their territory or home of a square mile or so. That may be so for a while with those stay-at-home whitetails but generally deer are no different than humans; when they start to get the small little spots on their face, neck and sometimes across the upper back, they get goosey and will roam up to ten miles. The more adventurous will hop across a state line for a night. Bucks avoid fighting with the old man this way and the more promiscuous does escape the domestic chores of the bedding areas.

As adults, deer must cope with the geometrically increased sophistication of the modern hunter, with the growing ranks of the trophy hunter, and with acid rain. Only the strong can survive in the post-nuclear woods and deer have no break in sight, no light at the end of the tunnel. There is hope in states like Wisconsin where deer are not seriously disturbed during the hunting season. There is chatter within the Zoological Society about turning that entire state into a national zoo. Early political test balloons, especially those flown in Minnesota, show positive response.

Veteran Deer

Survivors of multiple seasons hold reunions after each one closes next to the hunter parking lots to talk over the last season. The veterans compare notes, with the young bucks listening on, while the does prepare large meals of whole grains and berries.

All the latest tricks are discussed: the current camo, scents, deer stands, changes in regulations. Empty places around the circle are marked by small memorial piles of acorns and until everyone has a chance to get to the reunion, there is quite a bit of concern about attendance. Those animals with arrows still stuck in their haunches have them bitten off by the more junior animals with stronger teeth.

The season's best stories, told in a complicated series of grunts and bleats, are often accompanied by what sounds like chuckles, especially from areas with a high proportion of non-resident hunters.

Deer are normally very imitative. Noting the increased hunter use of mock scrapes and rubs, the veteran deer will describe their use of mock beds and trails to the yearlings. Pawing the ground to outline the area, the seniors will show where they plan to walk backwards next season and what inaccessible area to build their mock beds in. The elders will show spike bucks how to walk in moose tracks. Mule deer will show how to imitate a whitetail by lifting the flag and hopping like a rabbit. Whitetails will "mock-mule" by walking ten yards, turning around, walking ten yards, turning around. All veterans will discuss the fashionable methods of hunting and recount late into the evening memories of their worst case of "buck fever."

THE HUNTER

Types Of Hunters

The many types of hunters share basic hunting desires but are easily distinguished:

THE TROPHY HUNTER will pass up better eating does for a mangy old buck whose head will fit on the trophy wall and with magnum muzzles talk about their quest for the largest headgear. Their trophy scores are kept in some big book somewhere. Trophy hunters shoot trophy guns, wear only trophy clothing and have exclusively trophy hunting experiences. Without a trophy-sized listening audience, these hunters atrophy.

THE ORDINARY HUNTER is a regular guy, scratching to get out of the house and away from the ol' lady for a few days and hoping to get a taste of red meat to erase a full year of tuna casseroles and tomato soup from #10 cans.

THE ACCIDENTAL HUNTER acquires an animal by bumper-kissing a Bambi off a biway or by accidentally firing a rifle out a car window into a well-lit herd of night-feeders.

THE NON-RESIDENT HUNTER wants to be a local good ol' boy and will do anything to not only bag your deer but your wife too. They are identified by their new gear and each day in camp, wait for an overnight delivery of new catalog items for any late-breaking hunting strategy. In the local lounges, non-residents eagerly ask for the first dance and rarely make it to the last dance—more often they are the same dance, even with the ugliest local women.

THE CITY HUNTER is an escapee from some sissy white collar job, is terrified that he will do something wrong and makes a good "camp" girl.

THE RESIDENT HUNTER is recognized by his generosity to the non-residents and his willingness to share a favorite hunting spot, girlfriend or beer.

Preseason Activity

MENTAL PREPARATIONS: You should know what a deer looks like before you go tromping in the woods with dangerous weapons. Buck recommends multiple trips to the local zoo for viewing. Note the docile animals playing deer games. They will seem very content and well-fed, and happy to walk around in large circles.

Movies are a good way to get to know your animal. The Disney classic, *Bambi*, has produced generations of hunters, and neighborhood theaters will show great nature films on Saturdays at matinee rates. You can watch nature films on T.V., mostly narrated by khaki-clad naturalists. These nature programs are not hard to find playing opposite other sports programming, like the Superbowl.

Prepare for a deer encounter by purchasing a plastic deer for your yard. You can get a full size one that looks like the real thing as you drive real fast, practicing road hunting. It's one more way for the neighbors to know you appreciate Mother Nature, and the statues tend to class up the front of a house. They are more functional in the back yard where you can play wilderness games without being distracted by that bozo across the street, Herb, or policemen.

Realistic wallcoverings are available that show deer in natural settings and these full-size, four color photos look good in a living or dining room and prepare you for the woods. Find a trophy head at an antique store to hang in your bedroom. It's very important to fix these deer images in your mind at least three to six months prior to the season.

EQUIPMENT: It's not much fun to hunt without the right gear. Your friends will laugh at you. You won't be able to shoot a deer either. During preseason, you'll want to buy and use all the right gear to make sure everything fits and works properly.

Three months prior to the season, estimate what you'll weigh and go out to buy clothes to fit the new you. Your foot and hand sizes won't change much unless you work around band saws. Buy what you need and start wearing the gear as soon as possible.

Buck recommends wearing new gear, especially if camo gear, on your trips to the zoo, to see if the deer can recognize you. The gear may make you a little warm during these early months, but it's a good test to see if the miracle fabrics will wick away all that moisture. Wear the clothes while working in the back yard and call your little lady out on the back step to see if she can spot you. Wear your boots as often as you can. Like many commuters who wear walking shoes to the train, wear your Sorels and then change into work shoes at the office.

Wear your new gear outside to air out the store-bought smells. Some of Buck's buddies will bury their new gear in the backyard for a month or so. Then they will get a few gallons of swamp water from their hunting grounds and convince a new hunting partner to wash the gear with this natural water in his wife's washing machine when she is not home. This technique will really set the clothes up nice. If you add some heavier dirt and twigs, the clothes will soften up to become high fashion stone-washed togs.

Early in the fall, start gathering the old clothes for each upcoming season. Buck finds the most convenient way is to build piles of equipment in a handy place, like a hallway or sewing room, by season—one for duck hunting, one for deer hunting—capping each pile with the appropriate headgear. A recently used pile is easy for the little lady to smell out and handle as was spelled out in the wedding vows.

WEAPONS TRAINING: Get to know your gun early. Buck always says a man that doesn't know his own gun is not his kind of man. Practice taking it apart—in daylight, at night, in your bed. Take it to work disassembled and try to reassemble during boring sales meetings. Practice aiming it at inanimate things. If you have a scope, focus on the bedroom window of Herb's good looking ol' lady. You'll notice that the new, more powerful scopes can pick up very interesting low light activity.

The worst thing about shooting a gun is the noise and recoil. Get used to loud noises before you practice at the range. Have your impudent son set off cherry bombs in the garage while you are working and you'll know what opening day in Wisconsin sounds like. Have your wife sneak up on you and pop balloons whenever and wherever you least expect, particularly in the early and late hours of the day.

Most of the recoil of high caliber rifles is absorbed by your heavy hunting clothes. You can buy commercial recoil pads or have them built into your jacket but they always look goofy on just one side; padded on both sides, you'll look like a shooting geek. Just rip out the shoulder pads from a dress you don't like in your lady's closet and strap them on your body with Ace bandages. Heavy recoil can be prepared for by shooting that new elephant gun at the rifle range without your shirt on. This method will toughen those recoil muscles and if you wear a bearclaw necklace around your neck, the range master won't give you a hard time. For good measure, tell him the claws were personally pulled from a live animal. If you are an archer, put blunt ends on your arrows and pop off a couple at the zoo—it won't hurt the animals.

METHODS OF HUNTING: Buck recommends that you also practice your style of hunting. If you are a crawler, creep up on ol' blue death rattling through his last sleep in the back yard, circling to keep down wind, and goose him when he's least expecting it.

If you stand hunt, practice-sit a makeshift stand in the house. If you have a loft or second floor balcony, sit up there a full day, watching your little lady walk below. Perch outside in a favorite tree or on the roof and watch the neighborhood. Wear your new camo gear but it's more prudent to practice this technique in the back yard. Spend a full quiet day up there with a packed lunch, and carry on as you would in deep timber. Build your stand near well-traveled neighborhood trails. Remember, you are already near suspected bedding areas. Note any patterns of behavior. You may have several domestic pets join you but never mind.

If you are a stalker, start shadowing your bozo neighbor's wife as she walks to the supermarket. She will follow a familiar trail and is easily tracked in the neighborhood's natural terrain. The red high heels that make her calves so shapely leave easy tracks to follow. Like her woodland counterpart, she will probably stop along the way to browse. Give her leeway unless you want to see how skittish does get when threatened. Remember, these does can call a badge.

At the office, start on the scent trail of that new blond the boss hired. You are in full corporate camouflage and the tracking will not seem any different from other major office activity. Practice standing near water coolers or the major runways adjacent to elevators or potty areas. Get as close to her bedding area as possible.

If you are a ground sitter, practice sitting absolutely still on the floor of the family room occasionally watching all directions for unusual movement but concentrating on the sports channel. Test the latest electronic earmuffs that can filter out your wife's nagging but still allow you to hear the game. Avoid all eye contact with your loved ones. Deer consider direct eye contact very aggressive and impolite. Sharpen your hearing by sitting under Herb's bedroom window, listening for unusual noises.

If Lady Luck smiles on your first hunt, you should work on dragging skills. Practice dragging your wife or Herb across a yard full of obstacles on a piece of plastic. Your neighbor's wife would enjoy a good fireman's carry. If you expect to hunt in real cold weather, practice taking long naps in your walk-in freezer.

Preseason hunting is an excellent way to sharper your large animal skills. Unless you plan to flock-shoot a herd, bird hunting only polishes your shotgunning skills. An excellent preseason quarry is the wily grey squirrel. They have quick reflexes, fine senses, live in the woods, and can be hunted with rifles that don't make your ears sore. They scamper about the woods quickly and can fine tune your hearing as they scream squirrel obscenities from treetops. They can sharpen your eyesight by flashing small BA's before diving down a tree hole. If you are going to hunt them from a tree stand, make sure you have a ground partner or dog to chase them up your tree. Imagine the look on their face as they race up the branch that happens to be your leg. On those occasions, just pray that they've had their daily ration of nuts. Imagine the look on your face if they haven't!

Prepare your special part of the woods for a productive hunt. Make it easier for deer to get to your stand by bringing in a backhoe and carving out a path for your new friends. The larger and wider you make it, the more deer will use it. If you make it wide enough, you'll see whole families using it; fawns frolicking out front, followed by does chatting about common deer household things and the bucks not far behind, slapping two-highs about their latest rut.

Preseason preparations must include bringing in salt licks, fruit, and vegetable displays. If deer do like salt, there is no reason to think they will like other seasonings such as pepper. A herd decoyed like this is easy to track due to the sneezing but it soon wears off.

BUCK'S BONUS TIP: Once you think you have your preseason hunting legs, go to the hunting shows in full gear, sporting a name you made up for yourself, like "Mule Deer Mike." Walk by the big displays of mounted heads saying loudly, "Yeah, I have four of those on my wall." Tell guides that you have so many heads registered in Boone and Crockett that you must hunt under an alias. Don't spend a lot of time with the guides representing hunting camps because they are not really interested in helping you hunt anyway. They are only there to see city women with shaved legs and if you happen to show up on the second day of the show, look for love marks on their necks.

Hunting Widows

The oft-forgotten member of the hunting family is the lovely spouse, the ol' lady, the little woman, the "hey you, get me another brew!" The wife will suffer quietly through the preseason preparations; the emergency budgeting for those secret withdrawals from the joint checking account; the long smoky, beery planning sessions in the family room, and will bemoan her fate when she and millions like her become hunting widows during the deer hunting season. As their husbands back out of the driveway, they take their lonely posts in the upper windows and await their man's return.

Like widows who have just lost a wealthy but aged husband, hunting widows have short bereavements and usually recover by early evening to put on a new dress and head for the hottest bistro in town. There they will bask in the adoration of non-hunting Italians and other Latins, all of whom dance better than that oaf in the woods, either flashdancing by themselves or with a freshly painted, nicely scented widow woman on the arm. During breaks in the music, the lovely legions of the "abandoned" swear blood oaths of secrecy and usually arrive back home just in time to shower and smile out the kitchen window at the meat wagon pulling up the driveway.

Choosing Your Hunting Partner

The second most important decision you'll make in your life (second only to what caliber of rifle to buy) is your choice of hunting partner or partners. Your best hunting buddy can share your dreams, your plans, your table and if quarters are tight, your bed too. For all these reasons, you won't want to pick complainers, game hogs, lazy bums or out-of-condition jerks. This will eliminate your in-laws and immediate neighbors.

HUNTING WITH A WOMAN: The gentle sex have built-in advantages in that they are more intuitive and have better senses than you. A good woman can detect imitation scents on another woman, spot the differences between zircons and diamonds and overhear gossip that can cripple a career. They can cook better than Charlie too!

A girlfriend: This is one dear heart you want to capture, so show her what makes you tick. A trip into the woods might just seal the deal or then again might not.

Your wife: You are on dangerous ground here. How can she really appreciate your efforts by actually watching them?

Herb's wife: As head of the neighborhood association, it's generous of you to include Tammy and socially smart for her to associate with a local leader.

A camp wife from Vegas: A smart choice. Card tricks aren't the only trick they can turn for you.

HUNTING WITH FAT PEOPLE: In addition to their overwhelming presence at the camp dinner table, plump people need reinforced tree stands, tire too easily while driving deer, and will usually eat their lunch before mid-morning. They are usually more sensitive and make good camp "girls," although they use too much hot water during their showers.

HUNTING WITH SKINNY PEOPLE: Going back to biblical (even Roman) times thin people are not to be completely trusted. They are no good in a bar fight and can't pull out a deer under their own power. Their shoulders are too thin to absorb the recoil of a high-powered rifle and they spend the entire night rubbing Ben-Gay into the bedsheets. You can't borrow clothes from them and they have feet like women. They do camo well but their high-pitched voices screech across habitats.

HUNTING WITH DIVORCED PEOPLE: Hunting buddies with wandering wives suffer two ways; either they have been emasculated by the divorce court and lost all primal urges and would rather just sit and sob under an oak tree or they have regained their "stuff" and become over-aggressive, shooting more female deer than the law allows.

HUNTING WITH DISABLED PEOPLE: In most states, the handicapped are the only ones who can shoot from a motorized vehicle. Have your Vietnam vet buddies rig up a Briggs and Stratton on the chair to cruise the roads while you're driving deer out of their beds. A large "chair" with a tow rope is handy for dragging too. The handicapped are mobilizing with new organizations demanding handicapped parking, tree stand ramps, and hand bars over the slit trenches.

HUNTING WITH THE VISUALLY IMPAIRED: Responsible Wisconsin state senators have finally passed a bill that allows people to hunt who present medical evidence that they are unable to hunt alone because of blindness. This legislation was a compromise between the lobbies for the blind drunk and the just plain blind. Under this bill, a blind person can hunt and shoot if accompanied by a sighted hunter. The only requirement is that the rifle be painted white with the barrel tip red. The rifles are also outfitted with double sights and triggers similar to a driver education car. Once the animal is within "sight," the regular hunter will tap the blind hunter on the back of the head to shoot. For each time an animal is missed, the tap gets to be more like a slap. There is no clear limit on how many blind people you can take into the woods with you. Until all this is straightened out, Buck will not be hunting in Wisconsin.

HUNTING WITH HOMOSEXUALS: Attracted to the male bonding of the deer camp, these closet enthusiasts take a lot of group pictures to show their "close friends" back home.

HUNTING WITH PEOPLE OF COLOR: Buck's good buddy, "Big Scat" White, knows that deer can only see black and white and since black is thought to be the absence of color, he will hunt in only the skimpiest of clothes, usually just a codpiece. With this outfit, he has no problem attracting does.

HUNTING WITH ALIENS: States that share borders with a foreign country have special licenses for people who are substantially different from you and I and who have little regard for our laws and customs, especially when it comes to our women. Mexicans prefer hunting on burros. They are real good still hunters, hunkering under a large sombrero.

HUNTING WITH CANADIANS: These sort-of-English-speaking people are even more alien. They are required to hunt in pairs, one to carry and aim the gun, the other to yell "shoot!" They are highly irritable at being pulled away from televised hockey games and need help dressing in the morning in order to keep the zippers and buttons facing forward. For obvious reasons, Canadians are not allowed to hunt with, much less hold, a handgun. Do not allow them to hunt with hockey sticks.

HUNTING WITH EUROPEANS: The more violent Southern Europeans are best suited for blood sports and, if they can turn their guns away from their incessant family feuds long enough, they are good hunters. They are familiar with stuffing large dead things in trunks and are long disposed to using weapons to settle domestic disputes.

Northern Europeans traditionally turn their guns on themselves, particularly during the long cold winters. If a purebred Norwegian is hunting with you and you hear a shot, assume something or rather someone is shot. It's difficult for just one Scandinavian to put the long barrel of a muzzleloader into his mouth, but no problem with the help of a close relative. At the rifle ranges in Norway, rangemasters don't even set up targets. In Sweden, more bullets are needed because of near-misses. Scandinavians are raised to exhibit enthusiasm for nothing and it's only on occasional lutefisk overdoses that their billfolds will actually leave the baggy pants to buy a friend a cup of coffee. Germans really enjoy shooting at anybody, particularly the French, but only after a big meal washed down by kiloliters of warm beer. The French will hunt but they will only cut out the filets, leaving the rest to rot, and then cover them with some horrid sauce.

SPECIAL SHEILA SECTION: Buck has gone to considerable expense to research the habits of the woman hunter. He has left no stone under one carat unturned and this is what he has learned.

Woman has always been the hunter. The Greeks knew that first and then the editors of Cosmopolitan. The hunting skills of the lioness are the pride of the pride. Have you ever witnessed the opening hour of a women's shoe sale? You'd understand.

Women hunters will not shoot fawns unless they have a baby with colic at home. Career women prefer to blast does. If a female hunter becomes a trophy buck hunter, it's an indication of trouble at home or a blocked career path.

Your woman will want to let her body hair grow out. She has always wanted to do that, but make sure she shaves once home or she will want to hang around dope-filled coffee shops and talk existentialist babble.

Life In Camp

The different kinds of camps are directly related to the state of the bank account at the time of planning. There is an evolutionary scale of camps, but there are two basic types: outdoors or indoors, with or without a hard roof or as your woman carries on about, and with or without "facilities." Buck has tried them all and describes how your choices will affect your hunting day:

OUTDOOR CAMPS

On The Ground: J. Angus "Sourdough" McLean has laid a bag in many a hollow and dislikes sharing his nuts with the ground squirrels.

Avoid damp creek beds, sloped land, and caves with traces of bear breath. The single advantage of a ground camp is that it can be turned into a ground stand.

Lean-to: A temporary shelter at best, a lean-to is essentially a roof fashioned from tarp, canvas, a jacket, branches, or an old car door held up with rope, twine, or your belt. The leaning makes for fitful sleeping.

Tents: Cloth houses for sissies.

INDOOR CAMPS

Cabins: What you'd build as a hunting camp but as if you ran out of money halfway through, substituting linoleum for hardwood, and chintz for drapes, and installing no-name appliances. The mattresses are purchased from motel bankruptcy proceedings.

Motels: Distinguished by harvest gold shag carpeting and pole lamps. The front door is two giant steps from your front bumper. The more expensive motels have their own coffee makers and sanitized straps across the toilet seats; the less expensive have alarm clocks checked out at the office and a pay phone on the city light pole. The mattresses are purchased from hotel bankruptcy proceedings.

Hotels: If you are staying at a hotel, you are either not hunting, or hunting dears.

Lodge: Reserved for the Fortune 500, these hunting heavens must be taken in only small doses. Many of Buck's friends have stopped hunting after overexposure to lodge creature comforts.

Your choice of camp type will affect your behavior:

	Outside camp	Indoors camp
Toilet	Not allowed in bag.	On pot, according to seniority.
Eating	Hot foods over a fire. Cold foods in the bag.	If with a woman, in all the rooms.
Sleeping	In the bag, if you can.	As assigned by elders.
Drinking	In the bag, in the bag.	Everywhere.
Lying, boasting and cheating	Both inside and outside the bag.	Everywhere.
Puking	In someone else's bag.	Out the window, out the door, just out!

The hunting camp is a happy camp, free of domestic and professional concerns. Responsibilities are minor and easily managed within the hunting hierarchy.

The Senior Hunters, called *Stags*, have at least seven seasons and seven animals, five of which are bucks, under their belt and are entitled to:

> Sleep in single beds and get the extra blankets and pillows.
>
> Turn in the earliest, sleep in the latest.
>
> Get their choice of camp meats.
>
> Have camp coffee fixed their way.
>
> Belch at the table.
>
> Have priority seating on toilets.
>
> Hunt a day or so but may stay longer.
>
> Say "This food tastes like garbage!"

The Soon-To-Be-Seniors, called the *Velvets*, have at least five seasons and five animals (four bucks) to their credit and can:

Sleep in a double bed, get one extra pillow.

Be the first to say goodnight to the seniors.

Set the alarm clocks, inspect kitchen.

Belch outside.

Follow on the warm toilet seat vacated by a "stag."

Hunt extra days to fill out the camp bag.

Say "This food is a tad greasy."

The Intermediates, called *Spike Bucks*, have at least three seasons and three animals (two bucks) in the log book and must:

Sleep four to a queen size bed, five to a king.

Bring own extra pillows & blankets.

Pay deposits on cabin.

Hold belch, gas until well into the woods.

Eat what everybody else eats.

Hunt until they kill their own deer.

Say only "This food is a little cold."

The Juniors, called the *Buckettes*, are working up the ladder, aren't distinguished by season or animals and are required to:

Do all the dishes, drag out the deer, and dig latrines.

Sleep on floor if available.

Arrive first, wake up first and make coffee to order.

Brasso the bullets of the seniors.

Eat what the senior hunters recommend.

Hunt only as long as their dad can.

Say "This food is not bad."

The First-Timers, called *Bambos*, are the responsibility of the Juniors and must be seen, not heard. They are not allowed to have live ammunition and cannot eat until everyone else has had their fill. They will be the butt of many camp pranks. They will say "Is there any food left?"

Buck prefers hunting from camps that come with kitchens opening to living rooms with TVs connected to satellite dishes aimed at the Playboy channel.

FOOD IN THE CAMP: Indians used to prepare themselves for a hunt by fasting, hoping that self-discipline would make the animal gods reward their efforts with a big animal. The non-resident deer hunter's idea of fasting before the hunt is refusing the last beer in a half-rack. Oldtimers would eat what the deer were eating: a bowl of acorns, garnished with a sprig of honeysuckle for color, washed down by river water. This spartan diet reminded the early hunters of the world of the deer but was soon abandoned once they learned how hard it was to pass those acorns. Camp food is what your mother told you you shouldn't eat. Eat it anyway.

FOOD IN THE WOODS: Out there, nobody will know what you are eating, so all those things your whining old lady and family doctor have been warning you about can be eaten in peace and quiet. There are basically two food groups to be concerned with.

Food to feed the furnace: All the baloney sandwiches in the world lay at your feet. They squash easily in your game bag and you don't have to eat the crusts.

Food to keep you mentally alert: If you are standing in a tree in Northern Minnesota all day long, you should have a supply of candy and dry snacks to chew on to keep you awake. A long day can be partially filled by unwrapping the more expensive items. Try to keep something in your mouth all day. If your wife is with you, this shouldn't be difficult.

The Church Lutefisk Dinner

No deer season is complete without attending the annual hunters Lutefisk dinner. Normally held in the basement of the Lutheran church (or Catholic Church if the Lutherans are not back in from fishing), the annual fish feeds are a local food festival and out-of-town hunters are required to attend and eat all the lutefisk they can hold.

HOW TO EAT LUTEFISK

Pretend you have a cold and block off your nostrils. (It's not polite to pinch your nose.)

Swallow the smallest pieces as fast as you can.

Mash into the potatoes even though it is a shame to ruin good potatoes like that.

Hold chunks in your cheek and ask to be excused to go to the bathroom where, if there is any room left in the toilets, you can spit it all out.

Lutefisk will sit in a esophageal purgatory, halfway down your gullet, while your stomach lining has a chance to hide all its sensitive nerve endings. If you jump around a lot during this period, you run the risk of seeing the fish again and the odds are it won't taste any better going down the second time. Once the Scandinavian seafood hits your stomach, it takes about seventy-two hours for the fish juices and your normal intestinal juices to get to know and dislike each other. The explosive mixture will quickly change a still hunter into a typical non-resident hunter.

THE MENU

Entree

LUTEFISK
In a butter sauce.
In a cream sauce.
In its own foul juices.
(SWEDISH MEATBALLS *are offered to those who have a
letter from a doctor of at least one-half Scandinavian extrac-
tion certifying a lutefisk reaction.)*

Side Dishes

MASHED POTATOES *in a big bowl with butter,
and meatball gravy as an afterthought.*
CORN CASSEROLE *with Rice Krispies baked on top.*
DINNER ROLLS *with country butter and honey.*
Lefse too, but too closely watched to steal some for the camp.

Coffee and milk. No alcohol. Cider, maybe.

Settling into Camp

PRESEASON PREPARATIONS: Start saving for your trip
by secretly withdrawing funds from the joint checking account. Don't pack anything for the cabin that would give the
little lady an excuse to buy something new for the house.
Never let her go grocery shopping with you. Just tell her you'll
pick up what you need on the way and, once in the supermarket, buy what you've been wanting to eat for the last year.
Always buy extra Spam.

Listen to (but don't believe) the weather reports. A northerly wind to a meteorologist in a climate controlled sound booth is the breeze of his secretary refreshing his coffee. Look for ice on the lake. Send a junior hunter to test its thickness. That test will tell you how cold it's been.

ARRIVAL INFORMATION: When you are unloading your gear, hide your best food. If you leave anything good out, the oldtimers will bag it! Guaranteed!

Also hide your best longjohns and socks. In every camp there are a few sorry individuals who never bring enough and they are the ones that always have "accidents" in the woods.

CAMP MANNERS: If you are building a campfire outdoors, always build it upwind of Herb's stand.

If you need to take your gun inside, always unload it first—unless you are going to play poker after dinner.

HUNTING TIPS: Once you've washed your body with odorless soap, dust yourself with baking soda or maybe it's baking powder. Buck doesn't remember which but one will keep you cool and dry.

In the last days of the season when the hunters are slowing down, put a little Ex-Lax in the breakfast eggs. The increased toilet activity might kick up an extra animal or two.

If you have been the butt of many practical jokes and you are hunting a good distance from the others, shoot your deer, carry it out quickly and quietly along a different route and go directly home. It'll make a long season for your buddies seem even longer.

Drinking And Deer Hunting

Most states now require all deer hunters with drinking problems to wear blaze orange clothing. The laws vary from state to state, but there are mandatory percentages of clothing and the heaviest drinkers must wear more blaze orange than others. Some try unsuccessfully to hide their character flaws behind the new blaze orange camo.

There are a few ritual uses of liquor for a deer hunter. They are during:

The planning of the trip.

The night before leaving home.

The night before the Hunt.

The first night of the Hunt.

The last night of the Hunt.

Any remaining nights of the Hunt.

The first night home.

The drinking toasts are either congratulatory or commiseratory, offered by the senior members of the camp. They are as long as the attention span of the giver and about as interesting.

If you hunt in the back country of Georgia or North Carolina, you may run across one of those extra-legal liquor stores hidden where the moon don't shine. Just help yourself, taking care not to take more than your God-given right.

Buck does not drink while hunting as it's very difficult to keep a brandy warmer lit while in the woods.

HUNTING

Methods of Hunting

STALKING DEER: An active hunt which can be practiced by a single hunter.

Crawling is the preferred way to sneak up on a deer. It's estimated that the average crawler must cover over twenty miles a day to find a deer. Those miles are broken down into inches going over dead trees, through cactus leaves, around snake pits and swamp gas. There is no greater excitement, however, than crawling up on a deer snoozing in his or her bed, no greater surprise than when a quail explodes out of a bush in front of your face. Crawlers normally wear through several changes of clothing over a season.

Walking is the most common way to stalk. A successful walker must walk cautiously and carefully, making as little noise as possible. Walk ten paces and then stop and listen. Stay clear of brush that will scratch your new gear and don't step on big branches or fallen trees, no matter how much fun it might be. Watch carefully for crawlers. If you do fall down, don't curse like you do at home. Walk like a deer—on your toes. It's even better to move on all fours, like the animal, moving slowly, stopping ever so often as if you are having deer thoughts. While you are on your hands and knees, look under brush and low trees for deer legs.

If you have difficulty walking on all fours, walk with your buddy, at arms length apart, holding onto his shoulders. The front person will carry the weapon and is responsible for shooting. Walk in synchronized steps, ten at a time, taking short stabbing steps like a ballerina. This technique is very effective, particularly in an uncrowded woods, and can also help your ballroom dancing.

If while walking you see a deer out of the corner of your eye, keep walking. Do not look directly at the deer—they will bolt because of this aggressive behavior. Continue to walk calmly, mumbling about how you really don't like to kill deer anyway until out of sight when you can circle downwind and do them in.

Powerwalking is a more recent technique and the violent armswings are very effective for driving deer.

Chasing Deer is an old Indian sport and initiation rite. The sport includes running down a young deer, trying to get just close enough to hook an index finger under the tail and then put on the brakes. This is not a pleasant experience for a mature buck.

DANGER! You can get too good at stalking and making no noise and scare the bejesus out of a buck snoozing away the morning. Break a twig every so often and stop and grunt every fifty yards or so. The advance warning will be appreciated.

STILL OR STAND HUNTING: Whether at ground level or at some elevation, still hunting offers the purest forest experience. In a stand or blind, you can hear the cry of the whippenpoof, the tap-tap-tap of the red-headed woodpecker, the scurry of the field mouse, and the sound of a hunting partner going grunt.

Scandinavians excel in still hunting as they are always passively waiting for something good to happen to them. Native Southerners, especially those who are married to first cousins, come in a close second and the list winds down to the Southern Europeans, like Italians, who must be tightly strapped into tree stands due to their emotional outbursts.

In a stand, it's chicken one day, feathers the next. But the odds of bagging a deer from a stand are the highest of all lawful methods.

56

Ground Stands: If you are afraid of heights, you'll have to choose between a natural or a man-made ground stand. Natural stands can include just sitting against a tree stump or leaning against a rock formation. Buck prefers to use two special kinds of ground level stands.

The first uses the fact that a deer doesn't like to make direct eye contact with a human and is easily stared down. This is embarrassing, especially for the larger deer, and is the single most common cause of a "white flag." Buck likes to hollow out a seat in the dirt that puts his chest just at ground level and cover his legs with debris and leaves. This stand puts the hunter below the deer's eye level and is most effective in the dry Northern woods.

Buck's second most favorite stand had to do with a deer's diet. Deer really like apples, so one season Buck built a six-foot apple out of papier mâché, painted it red, and doused it with apple scents. Little piles of apple sauce, without cinnamon, were scattered within fifty feet of this natural blind and deer came from miles around to view this natural wonder. When deer gather around the old campfire, they still talk about their trip to the Big Apple. This noisy yet very effective stand only worked for one year and threw many deer off their normal feed, forcing Buck to switch to oversized pears and apricots in subsequent seasons.

Ground stands made by man are more varied, yet all share the common characteristic of being familiar to the deer; for example:

The automobile, truck or camper unit: In Minnesota, a hunter with high cholesterol can hunt from a parked vehicle but must roll down the window before shooting. Not so in Wisconsin.

Fishhouses pulled in for the hunt: Why leave your two-holer in the back yard when it can serve two purposes? Normally equipped with only a small stove and a hard backed chair, this stand is much like the home of a Norwegian bachelor and can keep you out of inclement weather.

There really is no reason why you couldn't pull in your bass boat as a stand. It has great seats and the multi-use will convince your wife of your economy. Deer in lake country are used to seeing bass boats too.

Biffy stands are a favorite of Buck's. Take the door off and face towards the trail. With a two-holer, you can entertain guests. Old restauranteers will put in a couple booths for even better seating. Buck has hunted out of a Barcalounger for years.

Tree Stands: Most of these stands are put up into trees and are commercially made or homemade.

First, you must pick your tree. It should be located about fifty yards downwind of a scrape or fifty yards upwind of a non-resident hunter in prime habitat. Look at the tree like you would a woman; it will be naked by the time you use it, so pick trees that will hold their leaves or better yet pick an evergreen.

Pick a full tree so you can take it home after the hunt as a Christmas tree. Don't remove the stand. Show your kids how you live in the woods. Bring a few red balls and some tinsel into the woods so you can both add festive spirit to the hunt and get a jump on decorating. Other hunters will think it a modern miracle.

Second, it should be a live tree! If this live tree is on government land, you're not supposed to attach any permanent nails or stands but then again, you are a taxpayer and if those high taxes don't earn you the right to pound a little nail, what will! You should pick a tree with low growth so deer can feed right under you, allowing for that rare pituitary gland shot.

Third, your stand should be high enough to be above the prevailing ground winds that could blow your stink around the county. If it is too foggy to see the ground when you climb up into the stand, yet you can see small aircraft, you've gone up too far. If you are hunting with a bow and arrow, an effective height is about twenty feet; with the longer range of a rifle it's ok to go up seventy feet or so.

Fourth, strap yourself in for a good hunt. Many will use a strong, yet stretchy strap that will allow a hunter to lean out from the tree to see what's coming up behind. Attach the strap below your neck and disconnect before you jump off the stand to go grunt.

Other Types of Deer Stands: There are many manufacturers of tree stands, all designed to provide a comfortable seat, with lightweight alloy metal and in full camo. Several models are like the tall ladders you used to fall off as a kid and look really natural to a deer used to climbing up on garage roofs.

There's no reason why you couldn't bring your own ladders.

There is no good reason why you'd want to sit on them.

Don't forget the man-made stand opportunities, such as powerline stands. Buck has seen many deer in places like powerline crosscuts near the Jack Daniels distillery and the tall cross beams holding the wires arcing the million-plus amps are comfortable places to sit. Okies and Texans use abandoned oil derricks as very effective stands.

METHODS OF GETTING UP INTO YOUR DEER STAND

There are several fast ways to get up into your lofty abode:

Climb up over a partner.

Climb up metal pegs.

Shimmy up the tree like a rope.

There are as many fast ways to get out of your stand:

Jump with knees flexed and a prayer in your heart.

Fall forward, taking care to first throw your weapon to your hunting partner.

Slide down as if the tree is a fire pole, aligning the knots where yours aren't.

BUCK'S SAFETY TIP: Always pull your gun up with a rope with the butt facing up and the rope through the trigger in case you have to shoot a deer walking under the stand.

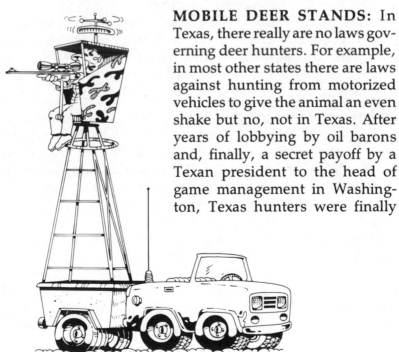

MOBILE DEER STANDS: In Texas, there really are no laws governing deer hunters. For example, in most other states there are laws against hunting from motorized vehicles to give the animal an even shake but no, not in Texas. After years of lobbying by oil barons and, finally, a secret payoff by a Texan president to the head of game management in Washington, Texas hunters were finally able to use their Chevy pickups to hunt game. Texans always take a freedom one step further, and started building deer stands on top of cars and trucks. Now instead of having to walk miles to a cactus stand, Texas hunters just have to crawl out of their car and climb up to an equally comfortable easy chair strapped to the roof.

Once strapped in, Texans cruise the deer beds, slowing only to take a more steady bead. During the hunting season, drive-in restaurants seem to easily handle the two level food service. Texans can build them as high as they want, taking into consideration only the low bridge restrictions. During off season they are used outside drive-in movies, high school football games, and sorority house windows.

Eating In The Deer Stand: It is a proven fact that body heat rises up through your head and out your hair into the cold air. Wear a good cap like Buck's and you can use the inner space as an oven, stacking and warming sandwiches on top of your head!

In this protected area, you can take the sandwiches out of their plastic bags, particularly if you've washed your hair earlier. There won't be enough heat to melt the butter but you'll want to be careful not to put too much mayo on the sandwiches as it's a lot looser. If you decide to heat your entrée in the quicker, hotter flame of your loins, leave the bologna sandwiches in the bag for sanitary reasons.

A TYPICAL DAY IN A DEER STAND IN NORTHERN MINNESOTA

One half hour before sunrise—Walk in, climb into stand.

Next hour—Wait for your overheated sweat machine to cool down and soak your clothes.

Next hour—Prepare to freeze your cajones off.

Next hour—Fantasize about your secretary.

Next hour—Fantasize about Herb's wife.

Next hour—Wipe nose on sleeve.

Next hour—Fantasize about high school sweetheart.

Next hour—Eat lunch.

Next hour—Fantasize about your brother's wife's younger sister.

Next hour—Go Big Job.

Next hour—Fantasize about business partner's wife.

Next hour—Wipe nose on other sleeve.

Next hour—Fantasize about last night's barmaid.

One half hour before sunset—Climb out of stand, walk out.

P.S. If you start fantasizing about your ex-wife, you can leave the stand early.

DRIVING DEER: The second most popular method of hunting deer is *not* taking a deer family out for a ride.

Deer driving is pushing deer into the range of a fellow hunter. This method is the more physically demanding but most time-effective in the harvest of deer. Some backwater states don't allow the driving of deer, but most civilized game officials encourage this fast-paced sport. There are two roles in driving; that of the driver and the stander.

The drivers are the more aggressive of the two and have to be restrained on occasion. A driver hangs aluminum pots and pans around his neck and ties a helium balloon to his cap to let the stander both hear and see him. The technique is to dress like a hockey goalie and throw yourself into the deepest and toughest cover that big bucks prefer. Drivers yearn to be standers and standers quickly become sitters and then sleepers. As you'd suspect, the most junior in the camp are drivers and try to recruit new drivers during preseason.

HILL HUNTING: 100% success ratio. The technique is to have hunters surround the hill, banging pots and pans with wooden spoons, forcing the deer up to where they want to be anyway, your pilot pals pop them off, for an easy roll down to your pickup. This method is most commonly found in areas with high concentrations of Vietnam vets.

HUNTING FROM A HORSE: The advantage in hunting from a horse is that a deer will think that you are part of the horse, admittedly the ugliest part.

Even though the horse's head seems designed to hold and center a high-powered rifle, Buck does not recommend, except in rare occasions, using the skull as a bench rest. Buck knows that the thick skull and relative brightness of a saddle horse should qualify it as a hunting prop and suggests that you should pull your gloves over the bronc's ears before firing and brace yourself for a second recoil.

Remember, horses have long memories and once shot from, should be given to the in-laws as bridle ponies. Other shooting positions include from the side, Indian style, or from under the horse, Hollywood stunt style. The second position, if not done properly, could make your friend Flicka another soprano in the Sons of Pioneers' chorus line.

If you're hunting alone, just let the critter go where it wants to. They like to run through deep snow or deep cactus cover where deer hide. If you're hunting with others, tie your bridle to the rear strap of the horse in front of you.

BUCK'S BONUS TIP: All four-legged big animals are kinfolk under all that fur and deer will come up to a horse to rub noses and sniff its butt. If this happens, lay tight to the saddle and shoot backwards.

HUNTING FROM A PIT: In actively hunted areas, it becomes necessary to seek alternatives to deer stands. Deer quickly smarten up and avoid areas that have trees that go BOOM. Mature animals look up, searching for ugly human growths on second growth trees. Many of Buck's cronies are taking advantage of deer walking around with their eyes to the sky by going underground. All that's needed is a pit deep enough to squat in, a screen thick enough to hold cover, and an active trail to place it in.

Have your partner cover your screen with twigs and dirt and brush the human footprints off the trail, then just wait for that trophy buck to stick his head over you.

HUNTING FROM A COMMERCIAL VEHICLE: Riding an Amtrak commuter train from Washington, D.C. to New York City one day, a graduate of Buck's Wilderness School became excited and popped off several rounds at a herd of whitetail standing in a New Jersey wasteland and was able to track his animal down several days later.

There are complicated laws regarding the discharge of firearms from public conveyances, such as metro and long distance buses and these should be carefully checked before you pack a piece for a road hunt. Practice common courtesy at all times. In the smaller buses, hunters should only use the window seats or the back row. Shots fired out a back window will be muffled by the loud diesel engines. When you stop to dress out the animal, it's traditional to offer the heart or liver to the driver or engineer. By federal law, the baggage compartments under large buses have been designed to carry at least six adult deer per compartment.

HUNTING FROM BOATS, CANOES, AND INNERTUBES: *Boats* are used both to hunt from and to take you to areas the less fortunate can only dream about. Commercial fisherman in Alaska hunt year round off their poop decks for unsuspecting deer coming down to drink near their illegal gill nets. Large boats are restricted to the more public waters but the new, smaller cigarette boats can take you right where the larger bucks have their summer cottages. Florida and Alaska-type boats powered by airplane engines are the trickiest to shoot from, since you are traveling much faster than the animal. Common practice is to flock shoot. Some states let you hunt from power boats only on private waters and almost never near public beaches when swimmers are nearby.

Canoes are a traditional native hunting boat. Young braves would stand on the bow of the boat, anxious to let their poisoned arrows fly. When they first used rifles, the recoil would knock them back into the boat, punching holes in the birchbark, and it wasn't until the invention of fiberglass that they were able to hunt like they used to. Some of our finest hunters, like the infamous H. Baxter, the Wyoming Wildman, use canoes to get to the dense cover along river bottoms and to those small islands in a river where the more prosperous deer have second homes. Islands and peninsulas are very easy to drive with two people—one pushing the animals to the pointed ends of the landform. Remember, deer should be completely dead before you put them in the canoe to return to camp.

Float Tubes or innertubes with a seat strap are very popular. Build a blind over your tube that looks like a little island. Much to their surprise, several old belly boaters have had deer swim out to their tube to browse on the foliage. The hunters slipped below and held the deer under until they yelled uncle. White water floating is the highest form of hunting adventure.

Should you be racing around a bend in a river and run right in the middle of a herd migration, throttle down and throw your anchor rope over the horns of the largest buck. This maneuver is great sport and will lead to all sorts of interesting events on shore. Don't shoot an animal in the water—number 1, it isn't fair or legal and number 2, the hole in the deer will fill with water and sink the deer. Let them reach shore where they will stand for a few minutes while shaking water off, or roll out of your boat on top of them like a Navy frogman, hog-tie them underwater and drift with the critter to the nearest sandbar.

HUNTING WITH DOGS: Dogs are used in Canada to track wounded non-resident hunters. In the southeast United States, dogs are used to push deer past pre-positioned stands through cover sooooo thick you can only shoot the smell of a deer. The cover is sooooo thick other hunters can't move about and these canines become your little driving partners. They are not supposed to catch the deer; their role is to slowly push them by hunters. The dogs are typically mixed breeds and the weapons of choice are shotguns loaded with buckshot. These hunting rites have evolved from coon hunts. Coon dogs are trained to push animals up into trees and, unless the branches are low, deer find climbing difficult. Opponents claim that does will drop their young during these chases and have added dogs to their list of timber targets. If you bag a free-running domestic dog in places like Appalachia, be prepared to stand in front of a front porch judge.

Buck requests that you respect the traditions of dog hunting by using at least a medium-sized dog—there is no reason to add insult to injury by using dachshunds or chihuahuas. Short-haired dogs slip through the brush best. Long-haired dogs pick up enough bristle to become camouflaged early in the day, but you'll want to keep these dogs apart at day's end because they will stick together and become difficult to kennel. French Canadians, always at the forefront of forest fashion, use lightly trimmed poodles for tracking, dipping them in camo paint for greater effectiveness. Anglo Canadians use pit bulls, training them by unleashing them in zoo deer pens while the zookeepers are counting the day's receipts.

Bird dogs have been used in deer drives but only those trained to point at upland birds. During the rut, a sexually mature dog will point at a doe in heat but not with its tail. Duck dogs are not much good after the first jump from the tree stand.

In the more advanced states, like California, you are limited to one dog per hunter. In less advanced states of mind, the number of dogs is restricted only by the occupancy of the local pound.

In the story of Bambi, our hero defended his new bride Faline against hunters' dogs and suffered a wound to the shoulder, confirming the old rumor that this part of the story was set in the deep Southeast. This makes sense, as old Walt Disney must have heard of this type of hunting when he was building Disneyworld down in Florida.

HUNTING LIKE INDIANS: Early warriors ranked hunting right up near warfare and handing out storebought cigars as a manly pursuit. Deer were hunted year round, according to need and most often by large herds of hunters. These warriors wore full natural camouflage, complete with actual heads and hides. Their weapons, according to cultural development, were spears, bows and arrows, snares, and traps. Once they had traded sufficient beaver pelts for smallpox and syphilis, they were able to lay their hands on guns. The dullest warriors first sharpened the end of the barrel and threw the rifle like a spear. There is no reason to think of the native as the best of hunters—they were just here first!

The most favorite native method of hunting deer was by drives. Most commonly, prairie fires were set to drive deer to water or other ambush sites. Tribes now extinct set their fires upwind of their villages. Fire "surrounds" wrapped a herd of deer with three sides of blaze, with the ambushing party at the mouth of the U. This technique had the advantage of providing pre-cooked venison. It's commonly thought by half the residents of Anchorage that it was fanned Indian campfires that set Bambi's woods afire.

Other types of drive included:

Chase to Water: You can't lead a buck to water, but a well-organized drive will certainly make him bob for bullets.

Chasing Over Cliffs: A technique made famous by old buffalo hunters, deer too were run off cliffs producing the first tenderized meat product on the market.

Driving Along Fences Into Enclosures: Trees were dropped along a line which created a ever-shrinking corral, pushing the animals into small pens where the warriors waited to take scalp.

According to commercial salmon fishermen, all the above practices are still being lovingly used on the major reservations.

DEER LODGES, RACK RANCHES, AND GUIDES

Deer Lodges: Buck has long dreamt of a trip to one of these privileged corporate enclaves, where the beds are softer, the meals less greasy, and cognacs and Cuban cigars close each evening. These lodges are almost always log, with huge stone fireplaces, chandeliers made of old wagonwheels hanging over a dining table covered by linen, decorated with fine silver and china and wildflowers in bud vases and groaning under a game feast that would humble Tom Jones. The chef is an accomplished hunter and knows how to capture the essential flavors of the day's hunt. The owner/manager can discuss with equal grace the custom guns of yore or the proper way to skin out a cape. The serving girls all have pretty little outfits, just a little tight across the bodice, squeezing the little darlings towards their chin. The wines are all fine and the conversation enlightening. While you may run into a bore occasionally, the other hunters are people you want to keep in touch with. It's to a place like this that Buck wants to retire.

Rack Ranches: In recent years, hunting-for-profit "rack ranches" have popped up all over the country, offering lazy city-dwellers and other ne'er-do-wells a quick opportunity to pass a lot of poor seasons for a shot at a trophy animal. These management areas are sanctioned by state and federal folks and are the logical extension of amusement park shooting galleries. As expected, in Texas they have special breeding farms run by newly immigrated Argentinians with thick German accents who are breeding does against their will to trophy bucks all in an effort to produce a "genetically superior" animal. These blue-eyed, blond-furred animals walk with an unusually stiff gait, as if in a march. In other rack ranches, spike and irregular bucks are culled early from the herd producing the first designer deer and yuppie herds in existence.

Guides: Due to pressure from guide associations, state game officials have slapped guide requirements on many non-residents and their money meters range from $100-500 a day, depending on the package. To properly check out guides, write the game department in the state you wish to hunt and from their approved list, write those who guide in the area you have selected. Ask them for references but more importantly, ask for proof that they do know how to bag deer—proof in the shape of a nice rib roast or several steaks from a recent hunt. This request will show how serious they are and if enough guides respond, you're well on your way to a full freezer. Politely ask for their ages and hunt only with the older guides who'll most likely get tired before you. Master guides are offended by gratuities; the best thanks for a successful trophy hunt is a warm smile and a firm handshake.

Special Methods Of Hunting

SCENTS: Your nose, compared to the sensitive instrument of a deer, is just a parking lot for boogers. You are naked out there, my friend. You can't smell a deer but they can smell you, and much before you come into range.

You have two choices; both of them good, and most effective when combined. First, you must mask your own stink, and second add scents that attract the animals. If you are Italian, the first job is much larger than the second. In scents, you are what you eat and all your vices produce an odor signature. If you have a par-

What You Smell
Like to a Deer

70

ticularly bad odor problem, cut yourself plastic underwear out of a large Hefty bag so your stink can't escape.

Masking Scents are available either from perfume factories or from your own making. Commercial scents are easier, but a smell appropriate for Wyoming may not work in Minnesota.

It's almost as easy to make your own scent. Scrape dirt that a deer has anointed into a glass jar, filling it half way. Take it home, add distilled water to top of jar, and let sit in a warm room for a couple days. Then filter out the dirt via an old T-shirt and use the remaining fluid as your very own custom scent. You are carrying on in the traditions of the great perfumers like Mr. and Mrs. Chanel and, if you do this right, you'll have to hoard these fragrances from your loved ones.

Attracting Scents are used by Type A, pro-active trophy hunters. There are two main types; one that smells like the food they like or one that attracts bucks to display their sexual or territorial dominance.

Food lures are hints of what a deer likes to eat: apples, acorns, corn on the cob and all these aromas can be bought through mail order. It's much easier to squirt on a little liquid lunch than haul in corn cobs or steal acorns out of squirrel holes.

Love scents are best bought commercially, as it is difficult for the average hunter to pinch off the love glands of a live doe. Storebought scents are tenderly squeezed from penned animals who have volunteered for social experiments. There is no evidence that their country cousins can identify city smells from these "kept" animals. A little deer musk liberally sprinkled around will make bucks think they are in deer Valhalla.

Where do you apply these scents? Masking scents should be applied liberally, as if getting ready for a date; behind your ears, a little spray on your wrist, a five day pad under the arm and behind your knees. If you are Polish or Swedish and know the difference, spray a little extra in your undershorts. Scents will last three days, so these "masks" might even linger until you get home. If the scent comes in an atomizer, have a buddy spray it on you. It also doesn't hurt to spray a little on a piece of cloth and attach to the back of your boots, wiping away your foot odor as you walk in. If you ate jalapeño taco chips the night before, spray a little in your pants before you head out.

If you are trying to attract deer, little scent bottles should be set out within range of your weapon. Place on fence posts, tree stumps, anything up off the ground because deer don't like to bend over a lot and the ground winds will help spread the good aromas throughout deerland.

New products are continually popping up on the market, even as Buck speaks. For example, there are smell "camo" tablets that you're supposed to take that will neutralize your insides by opening day. The tablets are being distributed by the Peace Corps to Third World countries like Germany where their national foodstuffs create toxic waste problems. There's even a new lubricant and bore cleaner that actually masks gun smells but due to the publisher's rush to get this book out, Buck couldn't get in his two scents worth.

RATTLING: During the rut, a buck can be called in by imitating a fight between two bucks, using either real or artificial horns. You can use horns you've ripped off of other deer, or buy artificial ones for about $25.00. A few of the artificial antlers are two right sides to prevent bashing your knuckles but smart deer can tell the difference—the resulting sound is as odd as two right hands clapping. Pieces of bones in a bag also work well. Just shake the bag for action. Be prepared for the unexpected. If you get good at this, you may have to defend yourself. A stag has the edge. His huge rack is firmly attached to 300 pounds of sweaty sinew while your little plastic horns are hand held and will seem inadequate in a long battle for turf. Many a good caller has had to apologize to an angry buck charging down the tarmac.

BUCK'S BONUS TIP: If you happened to bag an antlerless deer with your bucks-only license, strap your rattling horns on its head and prop the animal up in your window as you drive by the game check station, properly honking the number and types of game taken.

DEER CALLS: Many of the new breed of hunters are adopting an old hunting trick by calling their deer within closer range to be shot. This is done several ways:

Natural Calls: Oldtimers had to use what Mother Nature gave them and there are just a few left who can make calls with their own mouth. As you'll note, the new calls have no teeth in them and that's because these old guys either had no teeth or had broken dentures. Deer dentures aren't that good either.

Artificial Calls: A large cottage industry now services the demand for calls that sound and taste good. Most look like a duck call, are made from fine hardwoods and are packed with secret things. A few look somewhat like an auto-erotic device and should not be used in mixed company.

Mechanical Calls: In some states, you can bring a record or tape player to your stand, powered either by battery or by an extension cord plugged into your car's cigarette lighter. The advantage of these calls is you can turn them up real loud, driving the deer just crazy. The tapes and records of these calls are made at game farms under the most unhappy conditions. For example, the bleating or distress calls are produced by squeezing penned fawns too hard.

The types of calls are:

The Bleat: Usually done by fawns who are hurt, hungry, or lost; or who want to go to the zoo to see their city cousins. When you do this call, bleat like your kids at a toystore. The high pitched "meows" will break a doe's heart.

The Snort: A danger call and one you should pay attention to, especially if it's behind you. It is similar in sound to the one made by your mother-in-law when you described your dreams for her daughter.

The Grunt: A social call with three main uses; to call attention to an occasion, to tend a harem, and to be aggressive in a party situation. It sounds like your brother-in-law at his most intelligible.

Be alert, as all three sound like the fourth grunting sound—the grunt that signals that a large animal is moving his bowels. If you accidentally mimic that call, all the animals will think it's safe and will spend their entire day going toilet. D. "Snorting" Horton of Seattle once flushed out a buck while flushing out his own system and his wild woman, Dot, is still trying to get his clothes clean.

When deer snort, they are exhaling, forcing nasal wind through a dense forest of twigs and boogers. So, to mimic them, don't inhale! Blow through the call, aiming at the deer. Don't spit into the call; someone else might want to use it later.

To snort the natural way, wrinkle your nose, aim nostrils forward and blow real hard, taking care to lean slightly forward so your sinuses don't empty on your new gear.

You do have an obligation to know all the different calls, so you don't confuse the animals. For example, it's not appropriate to use a fawn call when you're surrounded by dry does. Experiment— try pulling in a spike buck with a dying big buck call, created by alternating grunts with heavy wheezing. Once you have mastered the calls, "feather" the sounds with your hand or a hankie to sound more sincere. When you strum the heartstrings of a deer, you will see its ears face forward, its tail awagging, and its nose up and sniffing for another furry friend.

Deer like all calls, however. If you are near a lake and forgot your deer call, use your duck call. It'll put the deer's mind to rest as the two like to play together near the lake. It doesn't hurt to put a dying rabbit or squealing squirrel call on the phonograph. Deer are very curious about how small animals die. The sounds are a part of a busy, generally happy woods.

A note of caution: If you are really good at calling, you may call in another caller. If caught in this situation, just slip quietly away so the other caller doesn't lose face.

ANIMAL MIMICRY: Late breaking technology regarding rattling and scents have brought the pro-active hunter even closer to his quarry. Some of Buck's friends will take the mimicking of animal habits a bit further.

Mock rubs and scrapes have been made possible by the easy availability of scents. During preseason, trophy hunters will take last year's antlers and deer legs into prime habitat and create natural signs, complete with the appropriate smells.

Mock beds are made by sweeping away surface debris from a likely looking spot and laying in the slight depression with your buckskins on. Deer drool while sleeping, so the research and development folks at the scent manufacturers are rushing drool to market.

Mock droppings are also available for a hunter's tool kit. Collected by feed bags attached to zoo animals, these marbles come with a juice to complete the gift package. Serious hunters will warm these pellets between their cheeks before placing them on a buck run.

Mock animals are the ultimate mimicry device. Buy a two-piece deer suit down at the local costume shop, use the latest scents made of dehydrated tarsal glands and droppings, and start your doe love calls. If it works, you'll want to be in the front half of the costume.

STAYING DOWNWIND: A forest of pulp has been spent telling you to stay downwind of deer to score. Do you realize how hard that is to do? Are those writers nuts? Some even suggest you build four stands—one for each wind direction— east, west, north and south! What if the wind shifts to the northwest? Next season they'll recommend eight stands and will double their consulting fees from the tree stand manufacturers. If you listened to all those armchairs, you'd spend the entire summer building stands. Buck is also expecting to see recommendations on heights of deer stands according to daily thermal changes. Nevermind. Build your tree stand like Buck's—wrap it around the tree so if the wind shifts, so can you.

UNUSUAL METHODS OF HUNTING

Each state loses a good percentage of their critters by methods not regularly listed. For example, West Virginia harvested 240,000 total deer in a recent year and of these, almost 11,000 were taken "non-seasonally." You can probably learn from these alternative style harvests. Here is the breakdown.

Automobiles (6800 deer): Detroit engineers have always added more weight in the front bumpers to help you harvest a steak off the highway. Your mechanical monster is an acceptable way to dispatch a doe to deer heaven. Aim to hit only the less tasty parts and hold real tight to the steering wheel. If you are on a busy street, don't field-dress the animal there. Throw it into your trunk and do the work at home. Some states require that you let someone know, but it's not clear which states these are or who you are to call. Some states are experimenting with reflectors that flash like deer eyes to put more animals near the center line. In many western states, this source of fresh meat has been the exclusive property of game wardens and highway cop families so be careful or quick.

Crop Damage (3046 deer): In agricultural states, if deer are eating your market goods, whether it be plantation crops, apple trees, or cannabis, you can take those hungry rascals at leisure. It doesn't matter if you own the property, all you have to do is occupy it and be able to prove to a game warden that crop damage has been done. If the damage isn't real noticeable, get a couple friends on tractors to trash the area like a herd of deer would.

Illegal (674): Poaching is a year-round activity in most states and is a spectator sport in most of the deep south.

Dogs (88): Near large metropolitan areas, huge bands of under-sized pets, all frustrated by being so small and ugly, chase deer for two weeks hoping to knock one down and then take another month to eat it.

Fences (54): It's not known exactly how to hunt with fences but Buck assumes that the weapon is those automatic fence gates, with heavy metal doors that catch and squeeze deer to death as they try to get to greener pastures. The introduction of remote control closures have allowed fence hunters to do well in recent years.

Trains (05): In northern states this is a much larger problem, especially as snow forces deer to higher ground. The cow catchers on the large freight trains damage the meat and the engineers will not stop the train for small run-ins. If there is a large "bump," the conductor will stop the train so that tourists can take pictures.

Methods Of The Hunted

Experienced animals have their wisdom and ingenuity to thank for keeping their headgear. After opening day, deer lose their happy innocence and will not stand still to be petted. All the horrors of the last season will be remembered and they will try all the tested ways to avoid meeting their maker.

CIRCLING BACK: Hunted deer will quietly circle back around the unwary hunter and come up close enough to sniff the hunter's butt. If you feel a wet nose, turn slowly so as not to scare the animal.

Young animals like party games, especially Peek and Bleat. They simply must know who the new creature is.

HOLDING TIGHT: Many a savvy animal will lay still in good cover when a hunter walks by. Many hunters, especially those raised on Disney re-runs, look only for standing animals.

There have been reports of trophy animals that have "held tight" so long that they cannot walk and have to be tended by other deer friends who bring water and regurgitated acorns.

Sometimes a mule deer will stand tight, thinking that you are expecting a moving animal but that never works since they can't hold their breath that long.

When pushed, big animals jump blindly into deep cover, thinking no hunter will follow. The evidence is loud crashing ahead of you and, if you listen close enough, you'll hear the grunts and groans of the animal hitting trees and hidden stumps. Smart deer don't bolt into tall timber—it hurts too much. If you hear this commotion, follow the animal tracks up to the edge and peer into the darkness—you'll most likely see a busted up animal who needs to be put out of his misery. The broken trophy rack can be made into buttons.

If cornered, a large deer will rush a hunter, and most state laws allow shooting in self defense if you can prove you warned the animal first.

Weaponry

RIFLES: There are long and short rifles. Short rifles have louder booms, longer rifles shoot further and straighter. Every deer book carries an opinion on what rifle to carry, so Buck is going to give you a little history and only one opinion and two maxims.

You really should carry a weapon that becomes you. If you are tall and lanky, carry a long lean piece. If you are short and stocky, stay home.

Buck's two favorites are:

The 30-30 Model 94: There were only thirty of these 30. caliber guns made in 1930 by a gunsmith named Wn.(short for Winifred) Chester who, in his mid-thirties, was considered an up and coming gunsmith. This gun is fun to shoot, especially in the brush, and can be carried in good looking leather holsters called scabbards that are traditionally tied to horses but can also be attached to motorbikes, A.T.V.'s, or your wife.

The 30-06: A much larger gun with a longer barrel. The ammo is very easy to find. Even the churches in small hunting towns carry it if you drop enough loose change in the collection basket. Buck carries it in bolt action as he kills with only one shot and is getting close to averaging *less* than one bullet per animal. He will fire a second shot only if there is another animal hiding behind the first and will use the same hole.

Buck prefers these guns mostly because they were given to him!

MAXIMUM MAXIM: The best rifle for you is the one you can best shoot deer with!

MAXIM #2: If your best rifle looks like a rag-tag pass-me-down, like Buck's old Springfield, leave it in the case while staying at a well-heeled game lodge. Buck takes a very expensive loaner from a gun shop to use signing in at the lodge and then sneaks out his old killer stick once all the hosts are back inside drinking cognac.

Scopes and Sights: Scopes are for people whose eyes, like their other body parts, are no longer what they used to be. They are single glass binoculars fitted on top of your weapons. The insides vary with different kinds of what's called reticles but all are expensive adaptations of crosshairs.

Some hunters will paste a drawing of a deer on the front lens and, when a real animal fills the outline, simply pull the trigger. If you like to shoot at greater distances just for the sport of it, mount your scope on backwards.

Iron Sights: These come as standard equipment on new guns and a gun shouldn't be considered a true gift unless there are scope mounts attached and another box under the tree.

Peep Sights: Standard equipment on military weapons; for the ex-military types who buy these relics, peeping is a way of life.

Bullets: Factory loads do not refer to the blue-collar union workmen that made them but to storebought shells, which are the safest to shoot. They are made under the tightest controls and are test fired under laboratory conditions at animals illegally purchased from unscrupulous zoo managers.

There is also an entire industry built around the reloading of your own shells. You can buy bullets, gunpowder, and shells from catalogs and custom build your own guided missiles in the safety of your basement. For the sake of your neighbors, reload your shells in a concrete basement and, if you are ordering gunpowder, ask that it be shipped first class for all the special handling the post office is known to deliver. Test fire your custom loads away from other people and tell your wife where you will be shooting should you be late for dinner. And breakfast the next morning.

Whether you're using your own reload or a factory bullet, you will want a bullet that slowly expands in the first deer, mushrooming to mid-size in the second and exploding in the third. The oomph behind the bullet is the gunpowder and the trick is to cram as much powder in as the cartridge will stand without blowing up. Your hunting buddies are always willing to try your custom loads so you really don't have to ask them.

Just put a few in their gun belt. They'll let you know how they liked them.

The oomph will peter out if the deer is a long ways off. The path of the bullet is called the "ejaculatory." The ejaculatory describes the rise and fall of the bullet from the time it's fired to the time it lands on the animal. This information is important as you gauge your shots. If the animal is too close, you may have to back up quite a ways to make a proper hit.

MUZZLELOADERS: If you like to wear buckskins and put grass in your moccasins, your weapon of choice will be a "smokepipe." These guns are loaded from the wrong end and have a bore that's as big as the one carrying it. There are small bore bores too. And, except for those who still wear coonskin caps while watching Davy Crocket reruns on the Disney Channel, most real hunters are puzzled by the enthusiasm for these popguns. It's estimated that there are more blackpowder hunters now than back when they should have been. You have a choice of using a flintlock, which is more authentic but more outlawed, or a percussion weapon. The original weapons are almost too dangerous and expensive to shoot so replicas are the common choice among these replica hunters.

The only thing muzzleloaders remember after a shoot is great clouds of smoke. By the time the mushroom cloud disappears, the deer, which was just out of the short range of this goofy weapon, will be in the next county. You can pick out a muzzleloader in a crowd by the surprised expression on his face and, more importantly, the powder burns around his eyes and nose.

Things to do while you're waiting for the smoke to clear:

> Go home and mow the lawn.

> Have friends over for lunch.

> Sleep.

Due to the short trajectory of a muzzleloader, most of these Kit Carsons shoot their deer lying down, oftentimes in their own bed.

81

There are several advantages to hunting with a blunderbuss. Game wardens think you odd enough to schedule a separate season. The wadding materials needed can rid you of old T-shirts. Novice shooters will shoot their wad too early. You get to use your purses for all the precious little accessories. Best of all, it's easy to find your deer, coughing their way into the swamp.

Muzzleloaders require perfect weather so the powder in the pan doesn't blow away. A flash in the pan best describes the social and hunting skills of these hunting romantics. Latecomers to the sport are now customizing their muzzleloaders with scopes. Some even have specially built Mauser actions to slip in once their fellow buckskinners are inside their tepees. Others will slip a modern handgun into the large caliber breech when the Kit Carson du jour isn't looking. They strive for authentic gear by using deerskin to cover a thermos bottle and hand sewing buckskin over their goosedown trousers.

The only verified cases of deer laughing are reported by oldtimers who have watched the animals peek over ridges overlooking muzzleloaders in make-believe rendezvous. Gnarled old bucks tell the younguns giggling at the camps, that's the way it used to be.

Muzzleloading is seen by respected sociologists as an attempt to regain our more innocent past. But when early settlers had a chance to use modern weapons, they threw their old muzzleloaders away.

SHOTGUNS: Shotgun hunting is required by law where wardens have determined that either there are too many hunters hunting too close together or that they just want to keep the more sophisticated rifles from a doltish local population who talk in single syllable words.

A twelve gauge shotgun is the most effective size and many states will set minimums for you. The range is fifty yards or less. Double barrel shotguns will give you twice the chance to miss an animal. Since slugs are the most commonly used shotgun, buy a specially barrelled slug gun and shoot slugs only. If you shoot slugs through your regular barrel, you'll have a wider choke for duck hunting later in the year.

OO and O size shot follow in popularity. If you plan to use buckshot, you must shoot close enough. To gauge the range, take your wife's buckskin coat, hang it on a clothesline and fire a few rounds. The charge will blow off a few buttons but when you think that the coat is normally full of muscle and tough flank steaks, you'll understand what ol' Buck is telling you.

In several states you can carry over/under guns, a shotgun barrel mounted under a rifle barrel. With this oddity you can walk the legal boundaries between the two weapon zones and fire in either direction.

The real danger in the use of shotguns is lead poisoning. So many deer are hit but not killed by shotguns that tens maybe millions of deer go the Big Swamp, dying a terrible death. After an adult deer has been hit by three shotgun hunters from Wisconsin, the poor beast is carrying enough lead to show up on radar. Constipation, fatigue and abdominal cramps quickly follow.

PISTOLS AND HANDGUNS: What with all the rifles that don't have a good home, there is really no need to hunt with a pistol. Action movies with short-haired heroes sporting aviator glasses have created a mob of pistol petes who have taken to the field. Thoughtful writers have nicknamed pistols "handguns" for the slower shooters who are not sure how to hold them.

Check with your local legals for permission to hunt with your Dirty Harry Special. Criminal law, not hunting regulations, governs handgun use and with over 20,000 laws in the U.S. governing the ownership and use of pistols, you have a lot of reading to do before you take to the woods.

When buying a pistol, order special barrel extensions from custom gunsmiths; the longer the barrel, the better the shot. Buck prefers a barrel at least thirty-six inches long.

Most handguns have an effective range of up to fifty yards. Hold the gun steady with both hands, or lean the barrel on a hard surface, like your wife's shoulder. If your hands are shaky from losing a fight with Black Jack, you'll need all the help you can get.

Pistols work best in deepest cover, and the hunter should have at least two properly holstered. Deer aren't bright enough to move faster than your quick draw and if they are city deer, they will appreciate a look at how the West was won.

BOWHUNTING: Bowhunters look at rifle shooters like fly fishermen look at bass anglers. Archers think themselves the purists, the practitioners of the "quiet" art. With a dismal success rate, they say they hunt more for the sport than the meat, yet have a wider support network for consolation and extended therapy.

Bowhunters work under all sorts of disadvantages. The ten percent overall success rate isn't strong enough to convince your old lady that you are really hunting while away from home. How does she know you're not just screwing around with your pals, coming home empty-handed with liquor on your breath and stinking from days of intense male bonding? How can you justify all the new gear? Game wardens give you a break with an earlier season, usually during warm fall days and in some states, if you didn't make a four-legged pincushion, you can still bag a buck with a rifle. The warden is under oath not to tell your fine furred friends!

To successfully bowhunt, you either must get closer to deer or have them snuggle up closer to you. Your own stink must be masked with stronger smells that are familiar to deer. For example in farm country, rub fresh manure all over your body; in deep woods, cover yourself with skunk cologne, freshly squeezed.

Remember sound moves faster than your arrow. The "twang" may reach the ears of the animal before your broadhead hits their broadhead. The final ignominy is when the a deer absolutely ignores not only your presence and your presents but tailflips a BA on the way out of range.

The traditional long bows are now being replaced by very sophisticated compound bows with pulleys, stabilizers, and scopes. The pulleys are designed to make it easier for these traditionally weaker hunters. Several manufacturers have

given their latest hi-tech bows to local native chiefs who are still on page one of the instructions. Another outfit is trying to build an over/under bow, with a high-powered rifle as stabilizer which will create a hole for the arrow to go in.

Like muzzlcloaders, bowhunters must beware of the urge to adopt the authentic weapons of their Cro-Magnon relatives. Flint is harder to find now and bows made out of saplings are splinter factories. It's difficult to buy the proper poisons too.

TRAPS, SNARES, AND NETS: These methods are not quite legal, and certainly not nice but they were perfected by white market hunters and are thought to be used on Indian reservations with great success.

Netting is by far the most popular, due to its relatively low cost. An Alaskan native can string a gill net between two trees and, placing a salt lick on the far side, snag those deer looking for a little more seasoning in their bland diet.

Equipment

Buck doesn't recommend any manufacturers and that's why this book is so skinny. Sportswear and equipment companies back their semi-trailers up to the homes of outdoor magazine publishers to gain a few favored words but Buck, while a bit underdressed, gives you the real skinny.

The best equipment you can get is your Dad's. The gear is free and field tested.

The next best set is whatever you can assemble out in the garage. Older brothers always leave gear behind, especially if they marry a city girl. Whatever you are missing, borrow from friends. Cultivate and keep friends with good gear. These people are always buying the latest stuff and will often forget what they loaned you. In fact, once you have borrowed gear, dye the material and stencil your name on. They'll never miss it.

The next best bet is to get down to the local Sears store for farm clothes. Don't go to one of the "new look" stores where the Arnold Palmer polyester clothes are pushing out the work clothes. Go to an old one where they may still have Ted Williams approved sports clothes. Old Ted knew his stuff, as did J.C. Penney and their brand names like Big Mac, Sears Best, and Carhartt are what separates the residents from the loud, overdressed dudes taking your favorite counter seats at the Tic-Toc Cafe. This sturdy wear, once seasoned properly, makes the best pass-me-downs.

It is really confusing to buy clothing and gear now. There are too many fabrics, colors, and sizes and it's all designed to make you dependent on other people's opinions, slipping into the odious realm of fashion. You have to guard against becoming an equipment maven. Buck had to ask one of the camo gunbearers behind a counter in a famous sporting goods shop as to the proper shade of orange for deer hunting. The lesson here is wear what you like. You can hunt in your street clothes. In Wisconsin, you can hunt in your wife's street clothes for all it matters. Many do.

The main thing is to be comfortable. If it's cold out, stay warm and vice versa. In Minnesota, the nine month winters are cold and the first things to freeze are your fingers, your toes (if stand hunting) and then your rest of body. If your kidneys chill down, prepare to die in the woods.

Buck likes wool: wool jackets, pants, outer socks, caps, long johns. Buck hunted in wool before it was pre-shrunk, when a wet stocking cap would bring on severe migraine headaches.

He'll slip on a cotton sock only if it has been dyed to look like wool. Buy thermal underwear like you buy a sleeping bag, in temperature degree ranges, but the best thing to do is go ask your mailman or a cop what kind of underwear *they* wear in the wintertime. Ask them in a deep, serious voice. Some "camp girls" will wear silk underwear, but be careful around them. In warm weather hunting, all this wool might give you prickly heat, so layer your clothing, taking items off as you warm up and dropping them along the trail to pick up on the way back to the truck. Trails of abandoned gear are a good way to determine how hard hunted an area is and, who knows, you might find something that fits!

Headgear is very important in cold climates since your body heat rises and a good cap will keep it in. Hair also helps, so start letting your hair grow out two or three months prior to season. If you wear a toupee, go to K-Mart and get a thicker rug for the season. Hairdressers in central Wisconsin are having a banner year in blaze orange toupees. If you are bald or balding, have a loved one put one or two coats of hard wax on your dome to help hold in the heat.

Footwear depends on the method of hunting. If you are tree standing in Minnesota, you need Air Force bunny boots. That need is as good a reason as any to encourage your younger brother to join the armed forces. Give him your shoe size as you see him off at the train station. If you are stalking, wear a boot that's quiet and comfortable, breaking them in at least a day before the season begins.

Good gloves for cold weather are hard to find. Buck has read all the claims, but ten hours in a deer stand in sub-zero weather will chill out any glove and what's more important here is the ability to slip your hands out of the gloves and down into your pants to catch a little body heat. An old trick to determine outside temperature is to see how far your nuggets have disappeared up into the ol' bag!

What to do for your eyes: If you wear glasses, bring along another set in case of breakage. Metal-framed glasses are cold in the winter. In high heat, opera glasses, while pretentious, are acceptable, especially in the hunting lodges in the Northeast.

What to do for your ears: If the loud noise of a gun scares you, you can buy electronic mufflers that amplify natural sounds yet cut out loud ones. If your eyes are really good, you may not need sound at all, so just wear a good pair of swimming ear plugs and you can belong to the newly formed "Four Eyes Only" hunting club. Similar to the fishermen who use lighter lines, these pros are hunting with their eyes only and often will one-up another by hunting with one eye closed!

What to do for your nose: An electronic nose muff has just hit the Wisconsin market so hunters can smell the kielbasa back on the camp grill. The "nose" will automatically shut off when pointing towards your hunting partner's Big Job.

OK, you are probably wondering what Buck wears to his Minnesota deer stand:

> A blaze orange watch cap to keep his sandwiches warm and meet minimum fashion requirements.

> A hand-me-down faded red wool jacket with a back game bag that leaks and a pair of no-name red and black plaid wool trousers that suffer from major fiber breakdown.

> A pair of blaze orange Gore-Tex gloves that easily holds the freezing temperatures.

> A motley assortment of hand-me-down wool socks and two full sets of wool union suits that nobody wants to borrow.

Psss . . . You folks at Filson, I'll mention your name in my next edition if . . . I need everything. Call me for sizes.

CAMOUFLAGE GEAR: Early hunters tried to hide behind trees and under bushes so deer would not recognize them. When that wore thin, they covered themselves with natural skins and heads. Military forces picked up on this childlike need to hide out and started big wars to test camouflage gear which is now available for sporting purposes.

What you look like to a deer!

Without Camo   With Camo

High fashion has slithered into hunting clothes and camo patterns are now available for most hunting habitats. The types are all protected by expensive trademarks and only the most secure hunters dare mix patterns. The key is to select the pattern of your hunting area. The very best is a new pattern called "mammoflauge" which features shapes of the two very good reasons why you had to get married.

Fashion designers along Seventh Avenue in Deer Creek, Minnesota are burning the midnight mink oil to bring you a new pattern called Resident Camo featuring stone washed, mismatched gear in odd, non-fitting sizes. Sportsmen no longer able to walk alone in the woods wear and weather the gear for minimum wages.

Several problems with camo: If you lay down in full camo for a snooze, stay away from the trail so another hunter doesn't sit down on you to eat lunch.

It's easy to misplace your camo toilet paper. Worse yet, it's easier to misplace *used* camo toilet paper.

It's difficult to see other camouflaged hunters which could lead to all kinds of archery accidents if archers could hit anything.

Camophiles even buy makeup, waxes, paints, and dusts to apply on their skins. Continual practice of these feminine habits has sent quite a few turkey hunters to Denmark for sex changes. Some hunters will camo their guns, the rigs, their old lady. Camophiles will dust their butt knowing that once you pull your pants down to take a dump, your cheeks look too much like a butt of a buck to that other hunter on the ridge.

BUCK'S BONUS TIP: Older, more conservative deer tend to see life in black and white terms so camo for these senior bucks is less important.

DEER HUNTING CHECKLIST

FIREARM	ARCHERY	MUZZLELOADER
Big Gun	Bow	Balls
Bullets (lots)	Arrows	
Ear plugs	Condoms	
Recoil pads	Quiver	
Ben Gay	Tricorn Hat	
Condoms	Moccasins	

HUNTING GEAR	PERSONAL GEAR
License (optional in some areas)	Footwear
Knife	Socks
Map	Pants
Condoms	Shirts
Rope	Jacket
Survival Kit	Gloves
Axe	Condoms
Radio	Cap, hat
Weber grill	Liquor
Scent	Custom cue stick
Wrist compass	Toilet paper
Chain saw	French ticklers
	Beer bottle opener

Camping gear is whatever you take to your Brownie cookouts: Tent, sleeping bag, shovel, camp stove, condoms, smokes, ice chest.

Woodsmanship

It is the mark of an experienced hunter to feel comfortable in the woods, with himself and with the terrible deeds of blood sports. Comfort comes from knowledge; from knowing what's right and wrong, and from experience gleaned from many previous seasons. Buck encourages you to mimic the senior members in your camp. Remember, you are on a vacation from a controlled and stressful environment. Relax. Enjoy. For example, while personal hygiene may be of paramount concern to your family and boss, in the woods it's a distinct disadvantage to smell like a painted woman. Get natural.

Buck has gathered a short course of tips to help you in all situations. The tips include toilet instructions, what to do when you get lost, and much more. He wraps up with a few calm words about buck fever. Many readers have written Buck about this woodsmanship chapter and said this advice has helped them even at home and work, especially the helpful hints about going grunt.

TOILET TIPS: One of the major difficulties of a deer hunt is how to organize trips to the toilet. The very thought of it frightens many a good woman hunter or camp spouse. What's most important is to know your body well and pace food consumption with your daily activity.

For example, if you must eat a big breakfast before hunting, use as little grease as possible so the food will hang in better until you have a more convenient time and place to toilet. If you do insist on larding up, eat as soon as you get up and, once finished, hop around the cabin to pack that food closer to the exit. Ten minutes before you plan getting into the car for the drive to the stand, walk around the camp, bending over often, trying to squeeze your intestines so they will work in the warm camp setting. If you are a senior member of the camp, the others will wait for you.

The next critical juncture is the walk from the car to the stand in the woods. Quite often, a bumpy ride in will start the desired chain reaction. Before entering the woods, look for a spot to deposit your used groceries. If you are in a large parking area, a very convenient spot is under the driver's side door of that sportsman who built his stand too close to yours. Cover your tracks with camo paper so it will be more of a surprise to him.

Without fail, the walk to the stand or the first mile of stalking will get results. Set your mind at ease. What you must understand is that the woods in which you hunt is really nothing but a big toilet. Why do you think they keep asking the question about where the bear in the woods go? The woods are a toilet for tweety birds, porcupines, little mice, Mr. Owl, ground squirrels, wild turkeys, and all the Disney animals. Express your natural urges.

Going #1: Several do's and don'ts for watering the lilies!

1. Do not aim upwind without wearing Gore-Tex.

2. Do not aim uphill without wearing rubber boots.

3. Do not aim at trees or bushes. These little antics will identify you as a competing buck in the eternal battle for territories and harems. A thick-necked stag will rattle your own antlers for your brazen behavior!

4. Do not aim near your stand or deer trail. To a clean-living buck, you already smell like a barge of Jersey garbage and there is no scents in adding to the stink. Wander over and water the stand of that bozo that foiled a good shot last year. If you can hold it, climb up into the stand and "whiz" all over his lofty abode. Do this when he's not in the stand.

If you are in a stand and don't want to or can't leave, empty one of those Ziploc sandwich bags and fill it for later disposal. Other containers that work are hot water bottles, heavy duty garbage bags, oil cans with spouts and, in emergencies, a thermos—making sure that this one is different from the one with the beef bouillon.

If you must go wee-wee, take your time and enjoy this break from a stressful hunt. After all, it's taken quite a bit of time to find that little fellow who's tried to hide behind layers of longjohns, especially those union suits which were put on backwards. Once you are finished, don't be in such a rush to put that rascal back. Several very famous sportsmen have told Buck that one of their greatest pleasures in the woods is to aim that little 30-30 in all directions, hip-shooting at that elusive trophy buck. Remember, nobody's watching!

Going #2: "Big Jobs" are major efforts, best done in camp or where you park your car. To be absolutely sure a bowel movement is in order, try to squeeze off a little gas and that will tell you how close you are to dropping the A-bomb.

Several important observations:

1. It'll seem like you'll never make it to where you want to go.

2. You don't know how much clothing you have on until you have to try taking the bottom half down in a hurry!

3. You don't know really how cold it is out until that north wind catches your southern exposure.

4. You won't ever know how silly you look.

5. It is very clumsy to shoot from that position.

Some other very important considerations:

1. Squat properly at a correct angle so you don't use your pants as toilet paper. Buck shows you how this is best done below:

2. Hold onto a small tree if an uncontrollable explosion is in the works.

3. Carry on and get the job done. The only remaining concern is whether you brought toilet paper. A wad stuffed in a back pocket several seasons ago won't do you much good now. A roll a few days old may work. A fresh roll is the sign of a happy hunter, especially one in the official colors, like blaze orange. If you don't have paper, your only choices are what Mother Nature provides or what you are wearing. In the case of the former, dry maple leaves work fairly well but "Mom" doesn't provide

much help in sagebrush country. Many new hunters will use these commonly found leaves:

Poison Oak   Poison Ivy

The worst case scenario involves the sacrifice of a glove, a handkerchief, or a pair of shorts.

BLOWING YOUR NOSE: Often during the most active times of the day, you will have an incredible itching inside your nose, way up there where you can't get a finger, even with your gloves off. Deer don't sneeze like humans so no matter what you do, try to muffle the sneeze! Remember, you will not just sneeze once. You will sneeze at least three times.

Option 1. Take off your cap and, pulling the edges tight around your nose and mouth, sneeze forcefully. This method will force you to eat the sandwiches going cold on top of your head.

Option 2. Pinch your nose real hard, leaving just a little passageway and inhale fast, trying to pull that ticklish rascal way up above the sneeze line. This hardly ever works, especially on opening day.

Option 3. If you are an experienced and happy hunter, you would have brought a handkerchief. Cup it in your hands and take the attack as best as you can.

Option 4. If you are new to all this and have less than average personal hygiene, pull your longjohn shirt up over your nose and let the thunderstorm run its wet course!

It's while cleaning up after a good sneeze that you'll under-stand why the old hunters wear wool jackets. Have you ever tried to wipe your nose on Gore-Tex?

Preventive measures can help avoid sneezes. If you are on a stand and you sense something going on up there, put one finger tight over the free nostril and blow hard, launching a mucous missile at the ground squirrel playing below.

SMOKING WHILE HUNTING: When smoking cigarettes, keep deer from smelling the noxious, burning weeds by walk-ing fast while you exhale so the smoke molecules will scatter. Throw butts only near a competitor's stand or break down the butt, tucking filters into a pants cuff for later disposal.

In the Southeast, where large fires in the tobacco fields hook young adult deer into a lifetime addiction, deer hunters can carry their ten-pack-a-day habits right into the swamps.

Pipes, stuffed with an aromatic tobacco, are enjoyed by all the denizens of the woods. As for cigars, the dime store variety with artificial fillers are not popular among non-smoking ani-mals. Cigars made from the original Cuban seeded plants are associated in the deer's mind with hunting lodges and the finer things of shooting sports.

Smoking local hallucinogens enhances an outdoor spiritual experience but will impart anthropomorphic characteristics to the quarry and therefore is best avoided.

SLEEPING DURING THE HUNT: You've been up all night drinking and lying with your pals or have slept uneasily know-ing that a "camp girl" would goose you just after you dropped off and you are just too tired to hunt all day. The early morning sun is sliding up over the horizon, warming you and your heavy, greasy breakfast and you just want to nod off for awhile.

First, who cares? Your odds of seeing, much less shooting at, much much less actually hitting a deer are so low it won't make any real difference.

Second, who'll know? If you don't make the mistake of walking back to the car and snoozing in the back seat, nobody will have a clue. Don't be obvious by sleeping along a road, trail, or logging path. Turn your face into the leaves if you plan on snoring. Here are some places to sleep:

Along a deer trail: If you are a light sleeper, you won't miss a chance to bag a animal here. The smart bucks will let you sleep but then again, odds are you wouldn't have seen them anyway.

On a deer stand: It's most important to tie yourself to the tree or stand so you don't fall out. Keep the rope tied below your neck.

On a drive: This is possible only if you are a stander. Don't worry about a little cat nap— the noise of either a deer or the drivers will wake you up in time to blast away.

BUCK'S BONUS TIP: Oldtimers like to curl up in a just vacated, still warm deer bed to snooze while the animals are out feeding their faces.

BUCK FEVER: This is a clinical condition characterized by acute twitching, drooling, glassy eyes, and general disorientation. Similar to shock, the blood pressure is lowered and the affected hunter is pale, with moist, cool skin, nausea, a bit of chest pain, and a rapid pulse rate.

When a large trophy buck enters an unsuspecting hunter's view, his bodily fluids change direction and produce this critical but treatable condition. The spooked hunter will often either freeze up in a mild form of catatonia or enter into hyperactivity, pointing and ejecting shells through his weapon without pulling the trigger.

The only proven treatment is to have the big buck leave the area. If the hunter was on a deer stand when the critter came through, you should look for him in the nearby bushes. Look for any broken bones or spirit. Occasionally there will be spotting in the hunter's underwear and this very human failing should be treated with good humor.

HOW TO ENTER THE WOODS: Most hunters only go in a hundred yards or so when they hunt but this distance can be like a football field full of Super Bowl monsters if you are not familiar with the terrain. Be brave. Wear a happy face. Wave cheerfully to your hunting buddies even though you are consumed with stark, bone-crushing terror. Here are two useful ways to enter the woods:

By Compass: Go to the tree closest to your parking spot, put your back to the tree, face the scary woods and take a reading straight into that darkness and start walking in; one foot right behind each other like you did in your last sobriety test for the highway patrol. Count the number of steps and at each interval, yell out 100, 200, 300 to set your memory. When you want to leave the woods, reverse the directions by just turning the compass upside down and follow the arrow out, walking like you entered, in the same footsteps, looking over your shoulder occasionally so you don't bump into other hunters.

By Tracks: As you go into woods, mark a noticeable path by breaking small branches and trees, carving tree trunks as you stumble through, or sprinkle corn chips, soap flakes or bird seed as a visible trail to follow out. This path will also help your friends find you if you get buck fever. Most recommended is to tie a string to your car door handle and unroll the ball as you walk in.

GETTING LOST: What do you mean, you're lost! Do you think Kit Carson or Davy Crockett ever got lost? You bet! They were lost all the time. History books can't account for over half of their days, so you know they were usually out in some God-forsaken spot, in a cold sweat panic, never knowing where their next meal or arrow was coming from. Songwriters couldn't string together the right words to describe their constant state of panic. But, if *you* get lost and admit it, your pals will think you are a goof-ball and never invite you back.

Ways to avoid getting lost:

1. Don't go in!

2. Be the last to go into the woods. After you are sure everybody is in, go back to the car and snooze out the day. One half hour before dusk, walk backwards into the

woods about fifty feet or so and start strolling out, singing happy hunter songs.

3. Never lose sight of a hunting buddy who knows his way out and stay just out of his sight all day, snoozing if possible and follow him out in the evening, catching up with him just at the road, saying "Well, that sure was some sort of day huh? See anything?"

4. If stalking an area, tie a rope to a tree in the clearing and circle hunt around the maypole.

5. If you forgot your compass, point the big hand of your watch toward the sun. Half the distance between the big hand and noon is either true north or south. If you are wearing a digital watch, point the crystal towards the sun and divide the second number by the minutes and that number will face you due south. Except for leap years, remember that the sun will always rise in the east and set in California.

6. If you are really lost, break the monotony of the woods and show real panic with primal screams, whistling, or shooting off a lot of shots.

Think now! Do you really want to be found? Do you want to be rescued by some granola-eating mountaineer who will make you seem stupid and helpless, who may take sexual advantage of you in your weakened condition and have his search dog dryhump your leg too?

7. Prepare to die. Dignity in these final minutes that seem like days is very important to you as a man. Your family would not expect less.

Hunting Ethics

IF ANOTHER HUNTING PARTY IS CROWDING YOUR HABITAT: Check out their stands a few days before season, making sure their tree stands are firmly attached, and/or birdhunt their area with dogs a few days before season.

IF SOMEONE ELSE IS IN YOUR STAND: Walk quietly up near the stand and fire off 2-3 rounds into the air. This is a proper introduction to your uninvited guest who will normally vacate the stand for you.

If there is a Mexican standoff and you don't feel like Pancho Villa, leave the area and wish the intruder a happy day. That night, drag an illegal deer to the stand and call the warden.

If that doesn't do it, declare the stand lost and sprinkle large amounts of deer repellant around the area.

IF SOMEONE ELSE SHOOTS OR CLAIMS YOUR DEER: Madness is an old Indian trick. The innocent natives believed that the Gods protected the insane and left them alone. Most hunters believe there is a base level of civility and if that is obviously missing in your character, you will have the run of the woods. Nervous twitching, drooling, and wild, rolling eyes all create nightmares for the pushy non-resident hunter.

Sportsmanship is the least effective judgement call. Game hogs have been cheating on their families and friends too long.

IF SOMEONE TAKES YOUR PARKING SPOT: Pull your old beater up tight between their bumper and the road. Slap on stickers like "This Car Is Protected By Smith and Wesson" and leave your meanest blue healer in the car with the window barely cracked.

IF SOMEONE TAKES YOUR WOMAN: There is little chance of that happening because of your loving, caring, nuturing relationship. Don't worry. If she is swayed by some smooth talking non-resident, let her walk. There are more in the woods.

IF YOU WALK UP ON SOMEONE ELSE'S DEER: Clean the beast up to the point of touching the really gross stuff— that way if they claim it, you don't have to do it. It's permissible to carve out a few filets for all your trouble.

IF YOU HAVE AN UNRULY CAMP MEMBER: The party license will permit you to gut shoot a deer for their share.

Where To Hunt

FEDERAL LAND: Saved for the hunting of immediate families of federal officers and political hacks on press junkets. These lands are managed by the Bureau of Land Management, the Forest Service and the Corp of Engineers and are vast land holdings that, like an Annapolis appointment, require senatorial approval.

MILITARY RESERVATIONS: These special permits require a short swearing-in ceremony and a short haircut. The permits are good for 2-4 years.

PRIVATE TIMBER: If you own or plan to buy a wood frame house, it's generally OK to hunt these acreages owned by the large timber companies. Hunt in recently logged areas as deer will congregate in the large, unattractive clearcuts. Follow logging trucks.

STATE LAND: Saved for the exclusive hunting of the immediate families of state and local officials, including judges, justices of the peace, sheriffs and state patrolmen. If another state borders your area, you may be in luck. Animals do not respect state lines except when crossing with another buck's woman.

STATE HUNTING AREAS: Where deer and antelope do not play! In Texas, for example, they took an aerial survey of the most inhospitable land combined with the fewest animals and reserved those 350,000 acres as a Wildlife Management Area/Public Hunting Lands Type II with special hunting fees required.

POSTED, PRIVATE LAND: You need permission to hunt on posted land. Write, call or just visit these yokels at home. If they can understand English, invite them to hunt with you. They especially like to drag out deer. All regulations say that your license doesn't authorize trespass but in some states, the fine print will show that the non-resident fees authorizes a day hunt on posted land if and only if you close the gate behind you. If you see cattle at the gate, let them out as the farmer would want you to. If a farmer gives you written permission, that document is legal and can be passed on to your children and theirs too. In some states it's legal to xerox and sell the permission to your friends.

NEAR A GAME PRESERVE: Have your little lady organize a large Audibon bird-watching group in the preserve on opening day and then road hunt.

IN A GAME MANAGEMENT AREA: Deer here may be wearing radio collars so just listen for your favorite station. You are asked not to shoot deer with radios regardless of how loud they are playing. If by accident, you bag a ghetto blaster, yell into the receiver to wake up the deer survey crew on the other end.

IN TOWN: The best place to hunt, usually restricted to bow and arrow. City parks, water reservoirs, school playgrounds, town squares; all of these should be hunted and hunted hard!

INDIAN RESERVATIONS: If you show receipts from tribal bingo halls and/or fireworks stands, you can hunt but only using their traditional methods. Game taken from reservations must have an official tribal document such as a stone with a sharp edge, a beaded leather codpiece or the keys to a turned over snowmobile.

IN DEER FARMS: Where the only most caustic food critics are allowed to vent their darkest natures by slaying deer in small corrals. Reports continue that financially strapped city zoos are selling mature deer to the highest bidding restaurant.

BUCK'S BONUS TIP: No matter where you hunt, go deep for quality hunting experiences. Like most vacationers, city hunters like to be within earshot of road and camp noises and the result is large herds in the direct center of any road-encircled area. In these epi-centers, you'll find herds only Jeremiah Johnson has seen.

IN THE MOUNTAINS: If you have the legs of a billy goat and the stamina of a long distance runner, mountain hunting can be productive and almost fun.

Conventional wisdom is to hunt a mountain side traversing at diagonals like these:

The object is to crisscross to a location above the deer, locate their bony heads with binoculars and blow them down with your bazooka. They love to play King of the Hill so the object is to get to the top first. A deer will not sleep on the top of a mountain as it can be very uncomfortable. You will have to get up very early to beat an animal used to playing this deer game.

Wrong Way   Right Way

If it's your first time in the hills, the traversing will make you walk funny. If you don't walk short leg/ long leg, you'll fall downhill.

If you walk only on one side of a mountain, your hips will slip out of alignment and lock, forcing you to forever walk with one foot off the curb.

IN SWAMPS: Nasty, stinky bogs full of snakes, leeches and, quicksand are where the really big bucks like Bambi's stag dad spend their retirement. Informal surveys by Buck's friends have found racks in these Golden Ponds almost triple the largest known Boone and Crockett heads, evidence of giants that have survived all trophy hunter tricks. The swamplands offer a large feast of plant life year round and efforts here will pay off. .

A good pair of waders or a wet suit is recommended for swamp hunting and the best stand is an abandoned beaver house. The way to find an empty hunter "hotel" is to convince your younger brother to bring his diving goggles during a

preseason outing. Hold on to his feet for a quick pull-out should he bump into Bucky and Betty Beaver coming out all dressed up to chomp through another forest. Crawl in, enlarging the inner cavity so the two of you can fit in there comfortably, back to back.

BUCK'S SURE FIRE REGIONAL TIP: If you have a large gator carcass, hollow the critter out and slide in feet first. If other gators slide on over for a chat, pull the jaws shut!

IN CORNFIELDS: Grainfed deer are prized table meats. Deer feeding elsewhere on sagebrush, cacti, and salmon taste like what they eat. Used to seeing humans in funny-looking clothing, cornfed deer are almost tame and, if full of sweet corn, are easy to hunt. During preseason, scout with a farmer friend by riding along on field chores, looking for fresh sign. In season, strap yourself sidesaddle along the John Deere like an Indian on a pony and shoot as you drive by the deer barn dance.

If your friend's farm machinery is tied up in bankruptcy court, practice still hunting. To "corn stalk," work a pattern back and forth, with the wind blowing across at a ninety degree angle. Always keep downwind, with the wind in your face. Keep facing the wind no matter what direction you catch yourself going.

Deer stands should be landmarks that deer can get used to seeing. Traditional approaches include tying corn stalks around your body, or disguising yourself as a scarecrow.

Aggressive young farmers will race along the furrows with combines and binders, sweeping deer off their feet and baling the critters. Small deer can be easily picked up, while the larger deer must be lifted with help from friends.

When To Hunt

THE BEST TIMES OF DAY TO HUNT

Before Daybreak: Some of the young bucks are just coming home so it's a good time to catch them with their buckskins down. The big bucks are snoozing away in the deep hollows, alphawaving through their own stag movies while does are trying to sneak out of the beds before the mature bucks rise.

Sunrise to Mid-morning: When ol' Sol climbs over the horizon, the grains of last night's feeding start swelling up and deer bellies start rumbling. Deer will get up, stretch, and go check out any new arrivals to the neighborhood. If that bozo Herb is just now stumbling into the woods, the deer will just lay down, knowing he'll pass them by or move out, avoiding an accident.

Mid-morning to First Hunger Pain: The time period is too short to be measured.

Lunch Hour: Deer move at noon because they know you are busy. They can hear the pressure release of the coffee thermos, the crinkly potato chip bag, the charcoal being dropped onto the Weber grill. If the hunting area is near a factory town with a whistle or bell, the animals know exactly when the lunch bucket opens.

Up to Siesta Time: Deer move even more knowing that you overate and that your senses are dulled by the high sun and a big belly.

To Dusk: Deer are now getting ready for their evening strolls along the boulevards and may want to get an early start.

In The Dusk: Don't worry about game wardens hearing your shots—just shoot three times even though you dropped that large shadow with one shot and yell out, "Help, I'm lost!" Gut quick and bury the carcass for an morning pickup.

THE BEST WEATHER TO HUNT IN:

Warm and Sunny: No matter what the oldtimers say, more deer are taken in good weather than bad; in warm, sunny woods like the movies, or landscapes freshly painted by itinerant Impressionists. These animals are at peak deerness, strutting along the heather highways. When they are at this high preen, blast them!

In the North, game officials set the opening day after being assured by staff meteorologists that the rifle season will coincide with the first ice storm of winter. Muzzleloaders and archers will snooze away the earlier seasons under an oak tree, waiting for a deer with sunstroke to trip over them. Buck will do his preseason scouting during the warm months, wearing his natural deerskin moccasins, stuffed with grass, so deer will feel comfortable, smelling the skin tracks of their brothers and sisters.

In the South, when it gets too warm, Buck strips down to his shorts to hunt, making sure to wear shorts with a button fly, not hot metal fasteners or an open fly that will let the Big Guy get a sunburn. Open-toed sandals keep toes cool, and a hat is important to keep the sun from frying the throbbing network of veins on your nose. Buck's chest is covered with rich, black, curly hair so he'll weave in some twigs and leaves for natural camouflage. When you walk in the dusty soil, drag and kick your feet to create additional cover. In the lush Southeast, it's OK to wear Hawaiian shirts with natural foliage—in fact, deer will acknowledge your fashion statements with quick, jerky nods of the head.

THREE DOE NIGHT

Cold and Stormy: When the barometer starts falling, deer start frenzy feeding, eating till they almost pop. Their stomachs will stretch, pressing their lungs north and their intestines south, producing shortwinded, constipated Type A personalities. Stand near these feeding areas but not too close because there are infrequent reports of thin-skinned big eaters exploding.

When a storm is about ready to hit, move to a location near the exit runways leading to the thick cover where they'll weather the storm. . . . Buck stood through one of the worst opening day storms in northern Minnesota and saw a lot of deer movement in that horizontal sleet storm; at least they looked like deer; at least they were something large and stopped moving once a few shells were lobbed at them.

Deer don't care about the cold so much. They don't get hypothermia. Cool weather actually keeps their coats from sticking too close. High humidity combined with cold temperatures will freeze sleeping deer to the ground and the animals must wait for the sun to hit their slope to start the day.

In really cold weather, deer will "pig-pile" on top of each other for warmth, with the big bucks on top. By shooting the top animal, you'll not only have bagged the largest beast but the carcass will hold the others tight for your hunting buddies.

In the Rain: Heavy spring showers can bring on a whole rash of childhood ailments like bronchitis and croup. Light rain produces grey, depressing days for the animal and the waterlogged deer will become morose and aggressively introspective. The associated suicidal tendencies do help the hunter willing to stand under an umbrella.

Rain will wash away many smells and the clear air will make the area much more dangerous for a deer. Deer will not bed in depressions in the rain and will look for higher, flatter, and dryer ground. There are rare occasions where deer have caught "cat-naps" in the back of pickup trucks while their owners were standing, soaking wet, less than a hundred yards into the woods.

If caught in a thunderstorm, stay "on the lake" like a good fisherman! Take care to keep your rifle barrel lower than your head. Electrical energy can flash across the sky to your iron peepsights and force you to leave your tree stand early, much to the animal's amusement.

CANADIAN UPDATE: In the eastern provinces, acid rain thunderstorms caused by the rubber smelting plants owned by the famous hunting boot folks will pre-skin a deer for you, making a difficult hunt that much easier.

In the Snow: Snow will push deer up from lowlands and down from highlands. It's most irritating to deer to have Mother Nature hide food like this. Deer will paw their way down to the frozen foods; frozen acorns are a very popular early evening snack (bucks like to hear them crack in their mouths) but most deer won't feed if the snow is blowing and covering their findings as they go along. The bigger danger is the chance of frostbite of the nose while in the freezer. Foolish fawns have had their noses frozen from this error and soon the black tip, like frozen toes, will rot and fall off, leaving the deer a life of sinus headaches and bad colds.

Deer will move from one area when the natural snow depth reaches certain parts of their undercarriage. This rude awakening causes the fourth kind of deer call called the hi-ho (bucks) or the shriek (does).

Some hunters say that falling snow makes deer blink more often which can cause rearend accidents. Falling snow does muffle hunters' footsteps and wise old bucks will lay down and curl up under the new white blanket. When you stalk in light snow, take care not to step on any large, live lumps.

Gale Force Winds, Hurricanes, and Tornadoes: High, heavy winds are terrible to hunt in— deer just hunker down since the woods become too noisy (and thus dangerous). Gale and hurricane force winds in Florida will, however, help in the hunting of the little lightweight Key deer found in the south but you'll need to keep your upland bird shooting skills sharp to hit them. It will be your only chance to take a deer "on the wing!"

During a tornado, deer huddle under trailer parks on the advice of unscrupulous mobile home salespeople. With their high center of gravity, deer caught out in the open are swept off their feet and carried for many miles, often across state lines into unfamiliar surroundings.

Medium to light winds make deer act like airport windsocks, facing the winds sniffing for that garlic sandwich you had for lunch.

How To Hunt

SPOTTING DEER: Deer are usually the only large thing moving about in the woods, except for that doofus, Herb. Sometimes you can hear them stumbling through the brush with dogs hanging off their back legs, or you may hear only the snap of a twig.

What you will rarely see, especially when hunting for white-tails, is a complete body. Experienced hunters will look for pieces of deer, an antler here, a back there. Train your eyes to pick out abnormalities in the woods such as horizontals where only verticals should be, shiny antlers and wet, runny noses. The moist, cry-baby eyes are a dead giveaway.

Remember, an ordinary deer is not much larger than your neighbor's guard dog. If you shoot a deer as large as a horse, you have shot a horse. The most important clue—most deer are seen with their feet on the ground. It's very rare to see a deer in a tree.

Deer Camouflage: Deer colors are designed by Mother Nature to blend in with their immediate surroundings. They do have a few difficulties.

When they shed their summer coats, the naked animals seem embarrassed and will lay dormant during this period. The new winter hair comes in early fall and is itchy during the first few weeks. The winter coats fall off in early spring and are quickly eaten by ground squirrels who enjoy the oversized hairballs.

If their coats change before the colors in the woods, the animal will stand out like brown shoes at a formal dance. The animal will once again go into seclusion until the colors co-ordinate.

Deer will do anything to break up their outline in the woods. They are commonly known to hide behind trees and brush.

What's not commonly known is that:

> Big deer will hide behind other animals. On a migration, a line of doe toe to tail will hide a big buck sneaking along the lee side of a hunter.

Big deer will walk on their back legs but only for short distances because of their congenitally weak ankles.

Big deer will stand on one leg like a stork if they can lean against a tree or another animal. Don't be fooled by this. There are few one-legged deer left except in Wisconsin where hunters full of "freshly brewed" stale local beer undershoot their animals.

All deer will purposefully walk through brambles and thickets to pick up of extra camouflage.

All deer will stop licking their hair during the season, knowing a spit-greased animal sticks out like a sore thumb.

JUDGING DISTANCE: There are range finding devices on the market but here too, Buck saves you money with a easy way to measure distance:

If the deer looks this big,
it's 50 yards away.

If the deer looks this big,
it's 100 yards away.

If the deer looks this big,
it's a long ways away.

AIMING AT DEER: You have to take a bead on a killing zone on the animal. Buck shows you below where to aim on an animal and passes on the clue that anyone hunting with a responsible firearm will get more deer by "low punching" the chip off its shoulder— it knocks a deer down and keeps it down. Don't shoot at the heart— it's the best camp meat and not polite to the romantic thoughts harbored within. Don't try to shoot the antlers off, they come with the carcass.

The state sport in Wisconsin is to "shoot the flag," right up the ol' "O" ring, carving out the filets and popping the spinal cord as the bullet, already tired, falls out the mouth. This "banging the bung" is very embarrassing to the mature animal.

SHOOTING AND DEER: No way getting around it, you will have to pull the trigger. The bullet will not leave the gun until the trigger is pulled, setting off a chain reaction with the firing pin hitting the primer and the shell exploding out the muzzle, looking for a warm body to blow apart.

The faster you pull the trigger, the faster the bullet will go out. *Don't* jerk the gun on these fast trigger pulls, you risk pulling your aim and hitting the doe. But shoot before buck fever sets in!

If the deer is running, don't shoot. These animals are really difficult to hit. It's best to wait until they stop. If you must shoot a deer on the run, lead the animal. A rule of thumb is to take the speed of the deer in miles per hour times how far the animal is away in yards, divide by the overall velocity of the bullet in yards per second, and multiply by the degrees in outside temperature. With this formula, figure out where they will be and just shoot at that spot—they'll be there in a minute.

If the deer is standing still, this is the position they expect to be shot in. Deer like to stand still. Mule deer think standing still is neat and actually hides them. The really dumb ones will even stand out in the open fields. Pick your best shot and blast away. If you are shooting uphill, aim up to a foot higher since bullets will drop some, taking care not to shoot straight up unless you want to knock off your own hat. If shooting downhill, aim a little lower since early in the ejaculatory, the bullet will rise. If you can't quite see the deer on the other side of the ridge, lob a few rounds over at a forty-five degree angle.

If the deer is laying down. . . shame on you for even thinking to shoot one in its own bed. Let the animal wake up in its own good time and then wait until it is well into its early morning exercises.

If the deer is kneeling, make sure that this posture is not some sort of animal genuflection to an animal god. It's not smart to interrupt a religious ceremony in the animal kingdom.

HOW TO SHOOT A WEAPON

Standing Up: The most difficult shooting position. Buck uses a very long sling which he can step on to steady his shot. Walk past a deer holding tight, put your rifle over your shoulder, aim backwards towards the spot the buck is laying, and pull the trigger. Due to the complicated nature of this maneuver, this is a one-shot event.

Sitting or kneeling: The closer you get to the ground, the steadier the shot.

If you hadn't noticed, squatting (called the "Big Grunt") is the most vulnerable position and, once mastered, makes you completely prepared to shoot in the woods, regardless of where your pants are.

Laying down: If you believe, like Buck, that this is the only good position, whether in a tree stand or not, practice getting down as often as you can. If you are a vet, it's easy. If you are a draft dodger, practice falling forward with a loaded piece. This position is more difficult with a bow and arrow. It can be done laying flat on your back.

As in all positions, use a bench rest, and that's another reason to have a woman hunting with you. Have her stretch out, belly down, in front of you and rest your large bore on her small bore. She'll appreciate the opportunity to help you score.

What to Shoot

Trophy bucks are not:

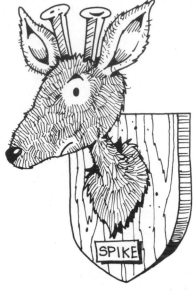

Button Bucks   or Spike Bucks

Trophy bucks have monster heads sporting mega-racks that trophy hunters spend all of their waking hours stalking just to get recorded in some dusty book called Boone and Crockett (firearms) or Pope and Young (bow and arrow). Named after the two flashy cops on *Miami Vice*, Boone and Crockett applicants are required to sign an affidavit swearing they fairly chased the animal through ten miles of bramble. Some states have their own Big Book which is jealously guarded by game officials who enter non-resident heads in pencil, not ink, to be erased once a local good ol' boy bangs a larger head.

You can score your own animal if you are able to understand the complicated point system or ask an official B & C scorekeeper to determine if your animal can be entered into the headgear hall of fame. If you're really pressed for time, send the entire head to the club. They'll clean it up for you and send back a mounted skull with a nice certificate. If you don't like the taste of venison, send the entire carcass. They'll appreciate the kindness.

Like their politicians, East Coast hunters exaggerate the size of their accomplishments by counting both sides of the head. In the West, the left side is the only count.

Trophy does are a convenient fallback for hunters who pass the buck. A new national club, Masters of the Matriarch, tallies teats for the record book. The old does are identified by their thicker ankles, saggy skin and big, floppy bags. Trophy does are always looking for younger bucks to service them (the harlots) and are nailed as they back through the woods.

Trophy fawns are a sophistication of the hunt for camp meats. Only those fawns with spots that measure three inches across can compete for these honors.

HITTING A DEER: You can tell that you actually hit a deer if you hear a loud splat (rifle or shotgun); or you hear the fifth kind of grunt (the "Oh, shoot, here we go again" grunt [bow hunters]); or you can't see the deer anymore.

If you are a muzzleloader, wait until the smoke clears before proceeding. If you are a firearms shooter, wait until the ringing in your ears stops. If you are an archer, start reeling in your arrow. A tug on the line means meat on the table.

When you reach the spot where you hit the deer and it's lying on the ground, make sure it's dead before you start carving out the chops. Lean over and listen for a heartbeat or pick up a leg and check for a pulse. If there is a slight pulse, time is running out. Hold one hand over the mouth and nose and then pull the lids down over the sad eyes. If the deer has just been stunned, take off your belt and tie it on like a bridle, leading the dazed critter out to the road where you can finish it off cleanly.

If the deer isn't there, you may have missed altogether or the deer, though hit, may have taken off to die more deerlike elsewhere. Tracking skills aren't difficult to learn. Just follow the blood trail slowly, looking for tell-tale signs of a wound, such as chunks of hair, a leg here, a tail there. Take fifteen minute breaks. Tracking is really easy in snow, more difficult in a late fall woods. You are getting close when the hoof prints turn into knee prints.

CAUTION: Veteran deer may try to trick you. Having dodged your arrows and bullets, they will limp away to pull you into a deer yard where the whole herd can rush you. These vets will even give themselves a bloody nose to make a blood trail.

PREPARING TO TAKE A DEER HOME

Field Dressing: Gut the animal so the meat is not tainted by the sandwiches the animal ate off your neighbor's stand. This procedure is fast and easy. Buck has gutted a deer in less than three minutes and has won awards at the national Gut-A-Ramas sponsored by the knife manufacturers. Gutting is easy, just turn the insides outside. After you are done, lean the stiffening critter near your stand as a decoy, beat your chest five times, and cry out the traditional camp chants.

Gut Piles: If you've done your shooting and cleaning properly, all the guts will be in a nice wrapped pile on the ground. A large deer's gut pile will be big enough for a small kid to jump on and will make all sorts of neat sounds when they do. Any size gut pile is a nice handwarmer on a cold Minnesota morn.

What to do with it? Some will leave it for the night animals and survivalists to eat. Some will bury it away from the prying eyes of hunting partners and game officials. It is important to take what you can use from this shopping bag of fine meats, in particular the heart and liver. These are considered prime camp meats and part of a traditional first night's meal at camp. Buck will usually leave the other parts where they lie unless there is a Goodwill drop box nearby.

BUCK'S BONUS TIP: Decide whether to take out the deer then or wait for help the next day. If you opt to leave the animal in the woods, protect your interests by "whizzing" a scent trail around the carcass. If it's a non-resident's animal and there's a chance of wolves in the area, it's considered good sportsmanship to "spray" directly on the carcass.

TAKING A DEER OUT OF THE WOODS: You are a non-resident rube if you shoot down into a valley. The deer won't come up to die at your feet—they'll find a deeper crevasse to fall into. Shoot an animal close to the road; veteran deer try to die as far from your truck as possible. At some point, you have to get your deer out of the woods. You *can* take the whole thing, by dragging or carrying. The most common drag is a drag. You'll soon learn why deer prefer to walk out of the woods.

For carrying, an Indian-style travois remains a favorite. It is, after all, the way a junior member of the camp brought you in.

Another familiar method is to put the animal on a stick and carry the carcass between two people. Ben-Gay was invented by two hunters using this method.

Most important, get someone else to take the deer out!!

BUCK'S BONUS TIP: Savvy oldtimers will cut up their animal into pieces and take the best parts out first. You run a little risk in losing the rest of the meat to other hunters or wolves but then again, that's the law of the woods.

Before you cut it up, undress the critter by removing its buckskin jacket. The skin can be pulled off by hanging the animal upside down in a tree, cutting around its legs and stomach, and jumping off the tree, pulling the skin as you fall.

HOW TO WEIGH YOUR DEER

Live Weight refers to the walking pounds. Most mule deer weigh a couple hundred pounds and most whitetails less.

Dead Weight is what's being carried or dragged by the hunter and is calculated at twice the live weight.

Dressed Weight can include the hide but not the gut pile and is about eighty percent of the live weight.

Butchered Weight is without the bones and junk and, depending on what a person calls junk, can be one half the live weight.

Dinner Plate Weight is judged by the acceptance around the family table, and averages two pounds per animal.

Butchering: This is the fun job. You'll learn what makes animals tick. You'll also learn how seriously overpaid union butchers are. Once you have the hair coat off, the critter looks like below (without the dotted lines and names)!

Chop it all up like shown below, wrap in double freezer paper and mark accordingly. Grind up any leftovers into hamburger.

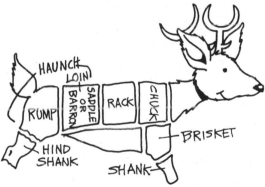

If you keep the head facing in the right direction, the other side will look exactly the same. Turn it over and complete the job.

If you don't have a dog, break the bones and bury them in Herb's flower garden.

HOW TO DETERMINE THE AGE OF YOUR DEER: Official party line says you have to stick your head in a dead deer's mouth to count and judge the wear on the molars. Buck simply cuts through a leg bone to count the rings. Who cares anyway? Your wife doesn't! There are more important things to talk about— like Herb's wife, for example.

Deer could live about seven years if left alone so figure one deer year is worth twelve people years. Except in Wisconsin, does will live longer than bucks— much to their dismay. Deer bodies will sag like yours; make a judgement call and stick with it.

You And The Long Arm Of The Law

BEFORE THE HUNT: It's time to buy a license and read the regulations. You'll need to memorize the arcane rules that will govern even your preseason activity. For example, it's illegal to put a permanent stand on government lands or in less permanent trees. You can't build corrals. You can't do this. You can't do that. It's like living at home all over again. Move out.

DURING THE HUNT: Hunting regulations are very clear—how many deer you can shoot, with what, and on what days. The real confusion comes in the proper hours of shooting; as complicated as game officials make them, you might as well hunt by tide charts. You can safely shoot a little before sunrise and a little after sunset. If you hear hunters shooting even a little earlier or later, they are probably just doing some target practice.

If you shoot an animal with a radio collar, remove it and attach it to the outside of your car for the drive home. Watching the big electronic map, the game biologist on duty will think that another deer has gone over the hill. If you bag several collars, it's possible to lure entire undergraduate study teams right into the city.

AFTER THE HUNT: Once your deer is tagged and ready to take home, you have just one legal hurdle to hop—the game check station. In most states, you must bring the game to the station by 8 P.M. or call the warden at home and promise to stop back in the morning. If you are a non-resident, you can leave your animal near the front door and be first in line the next morning. Game check stations are along all major roads pointing home and are often disguised as game biologist check points whose staff will ask you seemingly innocent questions. Evidence of the sex of your animal must be presented here. If you blew the head off, one or more of the following things must be attached; penis, testicles, scrotum and/or udder. If you are handy with a needle and thread, stitch a scrotum on a dry doe, especially if the biologist is an intern from a famous eastern school. If they can't tell what sex your animal is and you are hunting either a single sex license or area, the biologist will scold you and make you take your deer back to where you found it.

In some states, all that's required is to drive by the game check station and honk as often as the number of deer you have crammed in the trunk— long honks for bucks, short beeps for fawns. In other states, you will have to stop so game biologists can cut out the backstrap for their home studies on population densities.

Some states require a stop at the checking station even if you don't have an animal. This is so the officials can have a nice chat and serve the complimentary goodies your license paid for. In the morning, coffee, juice, and donuts are the usual fare; mid-day, a nice light sandwich and cup of soup and, in the evening, it's local beers, pretzels, and hard-boiled eggs. If the goodies aren't right out on the front counter, they are in the back. The officials are such kidders. Just keep pushing them; it's part of your hunting rights.

BUCK'S BONUS TIP: You have the right in most states to make a citizen's arrest should you suspect wrongdoing. Carry the largest weapon in these cases, seize the evidence, and tell the lawbreakers you'll be right back with a warrant for their arrest.

GAME WARDENS: It's a well-known fact that game wardens work for us taxpayers and, as busy as they are, they always like to be reminded who their real employers are.

The warden knows where the game is, so if there is a handsome single member of your party and the local warden has a daughter who's vulnerable due to her looks, unsettled marriage, or impending critical mass birthday, it doesn't hurt to gather a little information by penetration behind enemy lines.

Wardens will often give confiscated game or "mistake kills" to needy or empty-handed hunters. These animals are hanging in the warden's garage so visit early in the season while the good cuts are still available. Ask the warden if you can join him and his woman for dinner to sample the goods.

Game wardens get their legal authority from assorted hanging judges and in many states are no longer required to wear uniforms. They can be identified only by their well-fed appearance. If they *do* wear uniforms, notice how formal they look. If they look like stormtroopers, with high gloss leather and a Smokey the Bear hat, don't hunt in their state. Ditto for the states that employ volunteer Guardian Angels. These younguns are all graduates of the different mail order courses on game conservation and, as graduates, have pledged to produce the gilt-edged diploma when asked.

Wardens know all the game laws. If while shooting suds with pals at the Dew Drop Inn the night before the hunt, you have any questions just call the warden at home and be sure to let him know who's calling so he can thank you properly for your lawfulness in the stand next morning. It's likely that he just got in from spending the wee hours posting "Now Open For Hunting" signs on game reserves and is always happy to chat before settling down with the little lady who always wanted him to work for her father.

WRITTEN AND UNWRITTEN LAWS OF THE WOODS: The words that a warden can use to hang your personal antlers on his office wall come in the form of printed regulations. Each state has its own booklet of shameful secrets and unmentionable customs and will send you a copy if asked. If they don't want out-of-state hunters (like Iowa) or if it's a Yankee hunter wanting to blast away below the Mason-Dixon line, your request will go unanswered, be sent back without stamps, or be answered regretfully out-of-stock and told to check back later in the year.

The "regs" are printed with the smallest type possible on paper that smears easily. In North Dakota, regs are called proclamations due to the very large population of Missouri Synod Lutherans that hunt there. These thin documents are what the wardens pull out when your few rights are being read to you. Here they hide nonsense like not being able to hunt on Sunday. Can you imagine the chaos if deer start understanding what the difference is between weekdays and weekends? Why, we'd never get them to act like deer on a Saturday either! The Hawaiians have it together by requiring hunting on weekends only. The regs include definitions of everything; residency requirements, bag limits, license types. Some states will invent bag success ratios for each county to try to trick hunters into areas where there is low employment.

Generally speaking, if it's not prohibited, it's OK to do it! For example, it's fairly clear that you can hunt deer with falcons.

You will need to have some kind of license to hunt deer. Locals can buy their permits in sporting goods and hardware stores. Game officials try to pick the most frequented public spots so in Wisconsin, licenses are sold only in breweries.

There are several common types of licenses:

Resident: Reserved for those who have religiously bought tickets to the warden's ball, who have wanted to live in the state for a long time, and who have lived at least six months in a nice house with a well-kept lawn.

Non-resident: Must have three major credit cards with high lines of credit and must send a certified check six months before what's laughingly called an impartial drawing. (In some states, like Colorado, if you aren't drawn one year, you will get one accumulated point and two John Denver records. Extra points come from special relationships with certain game officials, and contributions to political campaigns. These points are added up for the season's draw.)

When applying for a non-resident license, the most common mistake is to underpay. Start off right, send an extra fifteen percent as a gratuity, to establish a relationship like with a maître d'. You don't have to be too clear on where you want to hunt. They'll give you the benefit of the doubt.

Sportsman: Reserved for special game management area hunts where special stamps or permits are required. Sportsmen must exceed all accepted standard sportsmanlike behavior in these areas.

Family Farm: If you are a land-owner, you can shoot as many deer as you can eat in two sittings. If you are a renter or sharecropper, your limits are the same percentages as your land lease reads. If you learn that a family farm is getting federal tax incentives, you as a taxpayer can hunt that farm without asking and enjoy the same limits.

Felons: As a ex-con, you are not supposed to possess, much less carry, a firearm. In some states, however, you are allowed to hunt with your parole officer, but only the parole officer gets to have bullets.

Youth: In most states you have to be at least fourteen years old to hunt big game. This is validated by the ratio of acne to smooth surfaces on face and neck. A youth must be a graduate of an expensive hunter safety class given by retired game officials that never liked hunters to begin with.

Lifetime: In Texas, you can buy a lifetime license even though there is no good reason to spend a lifetime there. These licenses are real moneymakers for states with high accident rates.

Deprivation: When animals multiply too fast, game officials will declare emergency hunts and allow hunters with fully automatic weapons to thin the ranks. All prohibitions are waived and all inhibitions are lost in these hunting horror scenes.

Military: Reserved for active duty personnel only, unless you're still able to squeeze into your dress khakis.

Alien: Reserved for Third Worlders. Because of all the mess they leave behind, these licenses cost fifty percent more than non-resident licenses.

Senior: If you are over sixty-five, most states will let you hunt free, but you can't go deep into the woods. If you are particularly forgetful, a special senior's warden will stop by to check your equipment before you go into the woods.

Party: These permits allow you to hunt with others and to shoot each other's deer. You can shoot a doe for a trophy buck hunter friend and, if the rest of the party is filled out, that's the deer he has to take home. For example, a party permit for four Wisconsin sportsmen will get four permits and a six-pack of Schlitz. Yes, they have to drink the Schlitz. Party licenses are sold behind the bars of 3.2 taverns all over the Midwest, right next to the pickled eggs.

Every license includes a tag to attach to your downed animal. This tag must be attached immediately after you shoot the animal and stay attached until you eat the whole thing. It's not as difficult as it sounds. For example, when you are boiling a leg in a pot on the stove, hang the tag over the side like a tea bag.

In a few states, licenses have to be sewn onto the back of a jacket or cap, in full view, so the warden can "glass" you from afar.

The big game license in a few states is the "senior" license and allows you to take as many smaller game animals as you can stuff into the deer's belly cavity. This deer license also allows you to take a bear if the bruin gets to your deer first and doesn't want to share.

In Maryland, you can apply for a big game license but must hunt with a "socially acceptable" weapon, following a lengthy approval process led by two schoolmarms, a school crossing guard, a librarian, a victim of a gun crime, and a billy goat.

If you forget your license, wardens normally carry extras so just ask for one so you can tag your deer. In the more service minded states, they will take "plastic." It's also very thoughtful to offer a little cash tip for all their help. In Maine, wardens will cash checks, up to $200 on out-of-town checks with two pieces of I.D.

Important Reminder: You can get a refund on a license if the game department made an error like misspelling your name, mistaking your sex, or housing you at the wrong address.

Some unscrupulous sportsmen will return their unfilled tags claiming small errors. Shame on them.

Or, if you die before the season starts. If you die of buck fever mid-season, you'll get only half your money back.

BUCK'S BONUS TIPS: Tag your deer in a spot that game wardens don't like to touch. You know where!

Fill your pen with invisible ink and let your partners use it before driving off to check into a game station.

HOW SEASONS, LIMITS, AND GENDER RULES ARE SET: Seasons are determined by the general activity of the deer and the desired harvest determined by game biologists. The recommendations are then passed up to the head of the state game department where they will decide on a number to compete with their buddies from nearby states. There is a lot of oneupsmanship as they scheme for the non-resident dollar. They will hold back publication of their own regulations until they can see what the neighboring states are doing. Without competitive information, the game heads will use random means like dart boards to set season limits. Buck has inside knowledge that Wisconsin game officials use the urinal roulette wheels attached to the blue deodorizers.

Game limits are, at best, general guidelines. In many states, it's the spirit of the law rather than the letter that is enforced. Just call ahead to the game department to find out which states these are. If you are allotted one big buck a year, this limit may be filled with two small spike bucks or one doe and a fawn. In several states, one doe is worth two fawns since twins are common in healthy herds and the spots are easy to draw a bead on.

Gender limits are used to balance a herd out. If there are too many does, they tend to get really crabby and picky about everything and should be thinned out. If there are too many bucks, the does complain about the double dating needed to satisfy the lust of the bucks and they too have to be weeded out. The best way to thin bucks out is to open their season when they are the hormonal heavies of the rut.

RULES OF BLAZE ORANGE: Except for a few small new irritants, like having to buy habitat stamps for special game management areas, there hasn't been much new in regs for years. But Buck has uncovered a scheme by several mountain states to add a migratory stamp for shooting mulies that move during heavy snows. This measure is small change compared to the new laws regarding blaze orange, specifically designed to fill the low occupancies in poacher prisons.

Game biologists, wardens, and retail clothing manufacturers have conspired to produce a report saying that blaze orange is the most visible color in the woods and therefore require that a certain amount of this obnoxious color be worn during your hunt. Blaze orange is already a trade name—what does that tell you? Many states don't even allow the more fashionable blaze orange camo. The only exceptions to these blaze orange rules are for farmers hunting on their own property and for bowhunters, again evidence of the powerful lobbies in Congress.

The language is noticeably ambiguous in most regs and very specific in some; it's hard to say which is worst. In Wisconsin, for example, the language is loose but ominous: "Faded or stained blaze orange clothing is unsafe and MAY NOT meet law requirements."

The minimum requirements are: at least some orange, visible from all sides. The square inch requirement runs from 150 to 500 square inches, worn above the beltline. The madness hits its logical extreme in Maine where they have forced their hunters to buy fresh gear each year from overpriced mail order catalogs because of regulations like these:

"Anyone who hunts with a firearm during open firearm season on deer is required to wear an article of solid-colored hunter orange clothing with a dominant wave length between 595 and 605 nanometers, excitation purity not less than 85% and luminance factor of not less than 40%. . ."

Now Buck asks you—Have you had your clothing wave lengths measured lately? Just go to our country's answer to Finland and have one of their Junior Birdmen quickdraw a nanometer on you.

MISTAKE KILL: If you or your hunting partner mistakenly kill any game you shouldn't have, most state laws require you to remove the entrails and deliver the carcass to the local game warden who will try to eat the meat before the next weekend. This restitution should be made within ten days as most wardens like a little aging on their meat.

If the accident is an extra deer or wrong sex deer, don't try to cover it up or cache it away for next season. Take it to the warden and leave it on his doorstep if he's not at home. Some hungry rascals will cut out the prime filets and chew the edges, saying the coyotes got to the carcass first.

If the accident involves a cow, horse or llama, you are in trouble. Check the brand and hope it's good looking as you'll most likely be wearing it soon, carefully applied by a couple of pointy-toed boots.

If the accident is an elk, moose, bear, or any of the endangered species, you are in bigger trouble. You've committed the big N-O and the FORCE is against you. Even your long family history of mental illness won't help you now. You and your next five generations will lose hunting privileges, always to remain a non-resident in your own state. You'll be stripped of your guns and the epaulettes of your new L.L. Bean safari shirt will be ripped off. They will take your wheels and you'll have to catch a bus home. The game wardens will go into your house and confiscate your trophy wall and make a serious pass at your wife. You'll never be able to wear blaze orange again except to Denver Bronco games. Your last deer stand will be on the reserved bench outside the whitetail display at the zoo. Life as you know it will come to a halt.

POACHING: Poaching deer is not a method of cooking; it's illegally taking deer that rightfully should be running by your stand. Recent evidence uncovered in Miami suggests that most poaching is run by out-of-country "save the little people" funds, usually headquartered in Columbia or Nicaragua. These organizations, with U.S. drop boxes in Delaware, are funded by empty-nester contract hunters to illegally harvest large herds. This enables them to force feed red meat to Third World children. It's been medically proven  that unwashed rice with large chunks of venison is the best diet to produce healthy adult cocaine smugglers.

Other poaching is done by those chumps in your high school class who still can't read road signs or who, in their quiet times in the tin trailer with a longneck beer, still think that school rules don't apply to them. These people still have their original crewcuts, widely-spaced eyes, and bad teeth and never could marry a high school sweetheart.

Poaching for antlers is for only the lowest of the low. Knowing that ground-up antlers are sold as an aphrodesiac, poachers will slay animals for their headgear alone. Game geneticists are racing to produce an animal whose antlers will cause city-wide impotence in Hong Kong!

Poachers are now being fined restoration penalties to replenish herds and these charges, tacked on top of the fines imposed by courageous circuit judges and justices of the peace can now total up to twenty or thirty dollars per person.

Poaching is usually done with spotlights that make a large animal's legs lock tight. In high poaching areas, it's smart to drive to your stands with just the parking lights on, so the warden doesn't mistake your high beams for two poaching spotlights!

Poaching as a Living: "Subsistence hunting" is a specialized type of poaching practiced most commonly in Alaska and other desolate areas by shirt-tail relatives of proud natives who settled the land or drop-outs from the traditional longhouse get-togethers. These accomplished subsistence hunters use the traditional hunting weapons of their ancestors, such as snowmobiles, air-powered boats, and fully automatic weapons and harvest enough food for a season weekly.

The original treaty rights renegotiated by courageous lawmakers grant the natives large harvests but only on the stipulation that they use all the animal body parts as their forefathers did. That's why you see so many three-piece buckskin suits in those oil offices in Anchorage. The natives are also larger eaters than their ancestors; based on their per capita harvest, each native eats just over five hundred pounds of venison a week, averaging twenty three pounds per meal, more on the larger Sunday meals.

A few subsistence hunters are back to nature enthusiasts, people on the lam from the alimony bounty hunters of Texas and Oklahoma who feel, in the tradition of Jack London, that giving up the comforts of civilization has earned them the right to pretty much eat as they go along. Well, Buck has researched this guy London and learned that not only did London not like to eat venison but that all those tales of the North were actually written in a north end San Francisco hotel and that the famous dog stories were actually about a bad-tempered chihuahua he kept under his bed.

BUCK'S BONUS TIP: With the new interest by restaurants in game meats, make sure you aren't ordering venison medallions from a poached animal. Politely, but firmly demand that the frog waiter hovering over the low neckline of your little lady produce a bill of sale from a reputable game farm. If he's unable to do so, leave loudly, using these French words of civic concern:

"*Hé, merde, ça schlingue ici! Y'a un salaud qui a pété! C'est degueulasse, je vais dégobiller. Les français sont tous des phallos. Connard! Va te faire foutre!*"

WHERE WARDENS RETIRE TO—CONFISCATION HOMES: Scattered through hunting states are state owned and operated homes to let wardens spend their last years free from the threats of poaching cabals. Wardens are recommended to the homes when there are collaborating reports of unusual behavior. For example, if when confronting a hunter, a warden displays trembling hands, sweat on the brow, and dilated pupils, and/or he gasps audibly once the animal is confiscated, he is a likely candidate.

From the street they resemble large retirement homes and are built as a hollow square, with sample hunting habitat in the middle. The inner square is designed for staff who dress up as hunters and carry illegal game back and forth so the residents can keep their skills sharp. The dining hall is decorated as a small town cafe, with counter service and older women dressed in short, white dresses, answering to names like Dottie, Ruby and Mabel. The coffee pot is always on. One half hour before sunrise until one half hour past sunset, the staff plays hunting cassettes taped at a local rifle range. The dark hours are accompanied by quiet environmental tapes. The front rooms facing the street are the preferred views and have crank-open windows for any deer drives that take place. These homes are supported by game warden fines and the United Way.

HUNTING IN CANADA: Regulations take a whole new meaning north of the border as you try to take your favorite weapon across the line.

> *What's prohibited:* Fully automatic rifles and machine guns, sawed-off shotguns, switchblades, silencers, mace, throwing stars, nunchaku sticks, belt, buckle

knives, spiked waistbands, blowguns, or brass knuckles. (The last prohibited item is very specific to a hunter from Michigan and is the focus of a class action suit.)

What's restricted: (With permits only) One-hand firearms (pistols, etc.), short semi-automatics like carbines, UZI semiautomatics if brought in for specific competitions, and terrorist class and special class rifles, like FN FAL.

What's permitted: Long guns are OK to import if you have the weapon totally broken down and stored in different parts of the car: barrel in trunk, stock in back seat, bolt in glove box, bullets in ash tray, *and* you have the same number of bullets for the number of licenses you have *and* you have at least $500 in "hard" currency and promise to spend it all while there.

Once you are in-country, you fall into one of three categories: resident, non-resident or non-Canadian, each with separate permits. The limits are similar and the prices are fairly reasonable especially knowing the prices aren't in real dollars. Do not make comments about the RCMP uniforms, no matter how goofy they look. Sergeant Preston will introduce his dog, King, to you.

Government officials make their own hunters feel good about their sport by making them buy various permits.

Permit to Convey: Required in order to take a restricted firearm, like a pistol, from where it was purchased to the local registrar of firearms for registration. . . even if it's the next counter down.

Permit to Transport: Required in order to take a restricted weapon from home to the repair shop and return, with a solemn promise not to shoot anything on the way.

Permit to Carry: Required in order to possess a pistol at the firing range, even if it's just to keep the spectators in line.

The provinces have their own special requirements.

In Nova Scotia, no hunter can take more than fifteen pounds of his deer to a neighbor unless the recipients have a valid storage permit issued by the health department and are good neighbors. You also have to eat your deer by April 30 of the following year or apply for a storage permit which is seldom given unless the hunter has a good reason for not eating freezer-burned meat.

Guides in this province are not allowed to guide more than three American hunters or twenty-five other Canadian hunters. No hunter can go into the woods unless "that person possesses a compass in working order and must be able to operate said compass to the satisfaction of any uniformed provincial employee not on strike."

In Manitoba, deer hunters can only include up to four people in a hunting party. Over four, you are considered an unruly mob (similar to their political parties) and subject to police harassment.

You are also asked to donate the reproductive tracts of the females. It's not clear what respected game officials do with these but the request smacks of improper behavior. The wardens even ask that you donate the hindquarters and backstrap for cadmium studies, whatever cadmium is. If you cooperate, you have a chance in a prize drawing for three dozen Perdue chickens and a bottle of Canadian wine, whatever Canadian wine is.

In Ontario, the game seal must be locked through the cartilage separating the nostrils, similar to the locking nose devices which larger Ontario women use on their men. Only residents get to hunt does. Since there are no limits on the number of dogs you can use to hunt deer, all the nightmares Cleveland Amory can have about this blood sport take place in Ontario. You can get a special cap from the Ministry in exchange for a suitably prepared deer hide for native peoples. These hides must be chewed properly by the license holder but the caps are well worth the effort. The caps do not have a bill on them as there was some confusion as to what side they should go on.

In British Columbia, dogs must be on a leash and the leash must be tied to the belt buckle of the hunter. Leashes cannot exceed 100 feet. In the la la land of Western Canada, you can take fawn mule deer as camp snacks if you have a special limited entry hunting authorization, whatever that is. If you hunt within one hundred kilometers of Victoria, you're expected to bring the field dressed carcass to the tenth floor of the government building so it can be checked off in the big book. Please use the service elevator.

In Alberta, you cannot shoot more than 200 rounds of ammo per deer.

In Saskatchewan, you cannot "aid or assist a Treaty Indian who is hunting for food in accordance with treaty rights unless you are also a Treaty Indian." Between the lines, this means dressed and acting like a Treaty Indian which includes most Canadian sportsmen.

If you have failed to retrieve a wounded animal after emptying your quiver, you can use your archer's license for the firearms season but only if accompanied by another hunter who has actually shot a deer with a rifle.

All hunters in this province must wear "a complete outer suit of scarlet, bright yellow, blaze orange or white or any combination of these colors. Your cap must be any one of these except white." These authorized colors allow the successful hunter to go directly to the golf course without changing clothes.

The fair trade agreement requires Canadian customs to keep the hindquarters of each Canadian deer as it's the only international transaction that they won't lose their arse in.

It is absolutely prohibited for Canadians to hunt while under the influence of American-made beer or liquor.

Going Home

TAKING A DEER HOME: Many states require a public display of your animal, in part because of smuggling and also as a lesson to other large animals. There are as many ways to display an animal as there are means of transport.

By Car or Truck: Some hunters like to pre-cook their animal by putting it over the front of their car. A warm engine in a warm climate will cook a full-size deer medium-rare in just a hundred miles. Turn the carcass every twenty-five miles.

By Train: The smaller lines have limited baggage room but are less formal. Don't skin the animal. Wrap the body tight with duct tape, strapping the feet tightly down, and shove the animal in the overhead compartment. Jam the tongue back in the mouth and tape it shut. Close the crossed eyes so as not to offend the other passengers.

By Plane: Airline people don't like hunters to begin with but what can you expect from people who have to eat airline food. They will always make you open the gun case that you have bound tight with duct tape so make it worth their while, buy an extra gun case and carry the gut pile in that one.

Buck debones a deer wherever he hunts and packs it clean and double-wrapped in a heavy duty garbage bag in a stiff, two-suiter. He will keep a few pieces out for a quick pick-me-up between the five course meals on board. If you have a full head mount to be taken back, purchase the adjoining seat for extra frequent flyer miles.

By Courier: Sensing an opportunity, several overnight carriers have told Buck that they'll soon offer a special "game bag" which can go directly to your wife so she can clean and wrap the meat before you get home. If you want the meat aged, ship it UPS.

EATING YOUR DEER: You are at home and again are the provider. If you followed Buck's advice, you have anywhere from 50-150 pounds of prime meat and are ready to eat venison, the red meat of monarchs.

Incidentally, venison is good for you. Deer meat is high in protein and nutrition, low in fats. It's lower in calories than a roast goose and larger too. Goose hunters are much heavier eaters and must wear oversized clothes. Venison is heavy in iron, which could put a little more lead in your pencil.

The preferred foods of our original citizens were the tongue, liver, and heart, and all the fawn meat they could find. A special treat was the buck testicles which passed on mystical powers of the deer: swiftness, sure-footedness, and a certain recklessness during the rut. Many personal names were adopted from this reliance on these venison vehicles, the most popular including Buck Rogers and Fawn Hall.

Is there a noticeable difference between doe and buck meat? Once you cut off the sex stuff, how do you know? An old deer can be tough but if it has been lying around the swamp for a number of years, it could be prime, especially on the side tenderized by its weight. A young animal will not be aged properly unless it's an only child.

CAUTION: If you haven't been eating much game meat, a sudden diet of it will upset your intestines and you can count on unexpected buildups of gas. These little pockets will slip out at the worst moments, so it's recommended that you eat the first few game meals alone. Once Buck floated a "fluffer" at dinner that was so terrible it made his older brother lose his dinner through his nose.

CAUTION #2: As one respected oldtimer warns, don't pass "game gas" near an open camp fire.

COOKING YOUR DEER: There are many cookbooks on venison cooking which are either very simple or very complicated. The complicated books are written by constipated unregistered aliens who follow the tradition of Europeans who ruin everything, with their fussiness and recipes that run over a page long. You can't expect better from a sub-continent of veneered barbarians that age their meat by hanging the game upside down, with guts intact. With their political leanings, they should serve borscht as a side dish. To cook "continental style" you'd have to own a commercial kitchen and be stuck with shelves full of exotic, equally useless herbs. Forget the food snobs! They've never won a world war and except for the French (who can't but should appreciate the irony), the Europeans haven't even lost a good "Asian conflict!" Never trust a recipe over a hundred words, including ingredients.

Cook simple. Buy all of Sylvia Bashline's books. Try Buck's recipes too! They're closer.

Buck's Venison Stew

Purchase 5 large cans of Dinty Moore Beef Stew.
Empty all cans into a large pot, heating to a slow boil.
Cook off a pound of your venison stew meat.
Eat the beef out of the stew before your guests arrive.
Add venison and lots of pepper.

Buck's Jerky

Leave your scraps out in the sun for week.

Buck's Venison Steaks

Cut your steaks an inch thick. Pour two inches of bourbon in your glass. Lightly butter a twelve-inch cast iron frying pan and heat up quickly. Slake your thirst with a couple more inches. As soon as the butter browns, lay in the steaks, cover with fresh pepper, and sear. Replace the two inches of bourbon. Quickly remove the steaks. Enjoy! It's not necessary to share the plate or glass.

Canadian Bakin

The traditional family meal of musk ox, beaver tails and wild yak milk can be replaced by any recipe above, covering the meat with maple syrup. Wash down with a warm Molson and pop a few maple sugar candy leaves for an after dinner sweet. Burp.

MISCELLANEOUS

Post-Season Activities

In the Woods: Be the last one out of the woods. You may find another person's deer or hunting jacket. In snow country, it's a good time to look for tracks and learn where the deer really were.

If the hunting was poor and you have a few cartridges left, thank the ground squirrels, woodpeckers, and blue jays that made your stand so quiet.

At Home: You will need to catch up on lost sleep. Since you work a full week, snooze during the daylight hours of the weekend. Hunters can take up to nine months to rest up from a hard hunt. When awake, your wife and her coffeeklatch will want to hear your stories. Often.

Back In The Office: Many graduates of Buck's wilderness course like to put certain deer organs in a glass jar to be placed on an office credenza, and hang the trophy head next to the picture of the company founders. By virtue of your superior hunting skills, you have earned the right to wear buckskin. Hair-on buckskin vests make a solid fashion statement in Denver and Salt Lake City.

The White Lies of Deer Hunting

We always see deer here!

I've never seen a game warden in this area.

You start dragging—I'll take over when you get tired!

I'll settle up with you when we get back home!

I'll be back with help!

That looks like a legal buck to me!

Try this—it's really good!

Naw, you don't need a license this far back!

I wouldn't take that kind of crap from him!

Loan me your knife for a while!

No, Honey, this is not a new gun.

Yes, Boss, I'll be back bright and early on Monday.

They'll never find it here!

I'm doing this because you're my best friend.

That's where I hit it!

It's in my other billfold.

What To Do With All the Spare Parts

The holiday season follows on the heels of the hunting season and no finer personal gift can be given to friends and families than momentos of a successful hunt.

The Hide: Turn it over to a professional tanner and into two gloves, two slippers or a sleeve for a nice coat. The quality depends on where the bullets went in and how many miles of dead stumps you dragged the animal over. Bullet holes can be made into button holes. It's not difficult to do the tanning work yourself, especially if your wife still has her own teeth.

The Feet: Cut from the leg and bent before rigor mortis sets in, these can be mounted on a board as a clothes rack for your mother-in-law.

The Antlers: To be openly displayed to the visiting public. In old times, the antlers were stuck back in the barn or garage but with the advances in taxidermy, it's now possible to mount the entire animal for a nature creche in the family room. Serious hunters will add brush and acorn displays to complete the deer diorama.

The Legs: Excellent digging tools for your child's sandbox.

The Skull: An appropriate desk ornament, the skull cap can keep paperclips and thumbtacks within easy reach.

The Teeth: Donate them to The American Dental Association so they can be polished and sent over to Third World countries as part of our Peace Corps Dental Assistance Program.

Hunting Insurance

Your regular policy will cover gunshot wounds if shot in a public conveyance—bus, plane or train. Wounds inflicted by beneficiaries are not covered. Heart conditions aggravated by buck fever are covered only if the animal was of trophy dimensions.

Special Policies: The N.R.A. and other shooting sports groups offer policies in their membership fees. The benefit limits are around $10,000 but are too general—for example, they do not pay a southpaw more for the loss of a left hand. One important loophole in the N.R.A. policy is that if you lose a hand, eye or a foot and wait at least 120 days to die, you can add another $10,000 to your estate.

Beneficiaries: Remember your hunting buddies. Don't add to their guilt for accidentally blasting you by not leaving them a little something so they can make it up to your family; especially your wife. A permanent tree stand in your back yard would be a fitting memorial.

Exception: Coverage does not include injuries sustained from the accidental discharge of a rifle while your toe is in the trigger guard.

HUNTING ACCIDENTS: Most states have very strict regulations regarding the accidental harvesting of non-resident hunters. Check your local regulations.

The Future of Deer Hunting

Some folks are asking whether hunting is really necessary. On the advice of National Park Service Rangers, these armchair anthropologists say that God will reduce the herd to its best level. Aligning with this school of fine thinking are naturalists recommending more natural alternatives of raising more wolves, bobcats, and mountain lions. Clubs of pit bull owners are also lobbying for more freedom in the field.

There is a new movement started by the asphalt industry and the used car dealers of America to cut more roads through prime deer habitat. By putting detour signs up at dawn and dusk, these entrepreneurs hope to bring the "road" hunt up to fifty percent of the total. The big insurance companies are fighting this in the halls of Congress.

Game officials are working hard with the latest technology to learn more about these animals so they can make rational choices in herd size and health. In an attempt to determine "maximum sustainable yield" of herd density, they attach radio collars and insert radio implants for tracking. By turning up the volume of the radios, they can listen in on deer doing deer things.

Officials are now more concerned about the quality of the hunt not the quantity. Quality time is the new buzz word in hunting. Like divorce counselors, game wardens will ask you if your hunt was as good for you as it was for the carcass draped over your fender.

Hunter Harassment

Anti-hunters are nipping hard at our heels, trying to take our weapons and animals away from us. The N.R.A. is trying to keep guns in our holsters, but hunters as a group have been subjected to all sorts of written and verbal abuse. We've been caricatured and stereotyped in the non-sporting press and this vilification has inflamed the inadequate loins of the anti-hunter activists.

The fanatics have decided to interrupt trophy game hunts by sending their most suicidal members to step between hunters with large bore rifles and their trophy sheep in remote locations. The organization behind all this has an international reputation for blowing up the wrong boats in foreign harbors and running into Ivan's whalers with rubber rafts. They chose rubber believing it's more natural than wood and enjoy the rubber nozzle that inflates the boat, passing it around like an old joint.

This good news is that hunters are finally getting their day in court with the recently passed hunter non-harassment laws. The new laws guarantee a hassle-free hunt and protection from the fuzzy-headed liberals who would hunt if only their women would let them. Furthermore, if a hunter sees a member of this pinko organization near his camp or smoking in a non-smoking area, it's now possible to make a citizens arrest for creating a public disturbance. Quietly but firmly arrest the offender and put it in your trunk for a round-about trip to the local constabulary. In a few western states, it's legal to spank the better looking females, however rare they may be.

The harassers are easy to identify; they are mostly aging hippies still asking what's called their women if 1968 was their best year, and driving beat-up, original paint Volvo station wagons decorated with SAVE THE WHALES bumperstickers. What's called men in that group wear turtlenecks and Earth Shoes, and have granny glasses hanging around their skinny necks. The men would rather be eating a bowl of granola than chasing pipefitters from Pittsburgh but their larger women and matriarchal mores won't let them. The women would come into the woods, but their open-toed Birkenstocks are a liability in a chase up the slopes.

Sunrise and Sunset Time Schedule

Except in Wisconsin, where resident hunters shoot both day and night, state laws consider a full day of hunting to start about a 1/2 hour before sunrise until 1/2 hour after sunset. Several states are considering 1/2 day licenses for those who can't stay put in their stand but until these exceptions are made, you're expected to put in a full day.

To determine the start of your hunting day, measure from the time guideline that goes through Buck's stand in northern Minnesota the distance to your stand and add five seconds for each mile west or subtract five seconds for each mile east or

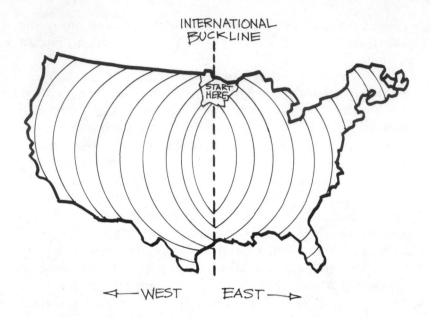

INTERNATIONAL
BUCKLINE

START HERE

←—WEST   EAST—→

vice versa depending on which direction you're facing. In Canada, add one minute either way for each kiloliter of Molsons you drink on the way to the stand.If you are driving deer east of Buck's stand, drivers must shoot first in the early morning but not required in the west. Legal sunrise and sunsets are listed below. Sunrise can often be misjudged with car headlights on high or full moon and sunsets are real tricky sometimes. On a long distance shot, your deer might be still legal while your shot is questionable! In these borderline cases, stay legal by shooting only in the direction the sun is moving.

International Buckline

Sunrise: October 01 to December 31, any year.

Starts at 7:11 A.M. ends at 7:56 A.M.

Except for late October/early November when the clock is set back an hour for breakfast, add a minute a day or so to determine the legal sunrise.

Sunset: October 01 to December 31, any year.

Starts at 6:54 P.M. ends at 4:34 P.M.

Allowing for a dinner break mid-season, subtract a minute or so each day.

Excuses

Before you go into the woods, decide if you really want to shoot an animal. If by some genetic mistake, you can't do it, here is a mitfull of excuses you can drag out!

In the Camp

> Nope. Didn't see nothing. Nope.
>
> Nope. Didn't hear nothing. Nope.
>
> Too cold, warm, wet, dry, windy, snowy.
>
> Won't shoot a flag!
>
> All I saw was does (bucks only area).
>
> That stand has never been good.
>
> Was taking a dump.

At Home

> All I saw was fawns (to children).
>
> Couldn't get a clean shot.
>
> All I saw was does (to wife).
>
> Too cold, warm, wet, dry, windy, snowy.
>
> One more day would have done it but wanted to come home to: see my honey, my kids, mow the lawn, clean the garage.

Don't Say: "My heart just wasn't in it." You'll never get out of the house again. Might just as well tie her apron strings to your belt buckle.

The Big Secret

Don't let your wife read this part of the book!

If your hunting expeditions are still being sold as bringing home the bacon, you now only have to walk as far as your corner telephone booth. Yup, what you've scaled mountains, humped hedgerows and sat in cold, creaky deer stands for is now available through mail order. All you need is a quarter to reach out and touch your favorite quarry. Thanks to modern animal husbandry and a quickening interest for game meat in fine restaurants, your furred friends can be ordered like you order pizza—by phone.

Originally designed as a convenience to institutional food buyers, the new consumer service can be habit-forming for those who chill too quickly, whose joints ache after a day pounding cornfields, whose eyes no longer coordinate with the trigger finger. Of course, the terrible temptation would be to pack up as usual, kiss the loved ones good-by, drive directly to the local flashing BUD LITE sign to call in your orders and just hole up with your cronies for a long carousing weekend!

No guilt, though! You are still the provider, still hunting for wild game . . . in the selection of the right distributor!

Remember how you are the target of that annual "zinger" about how expensive game meat is once all the bills are tallied? Well, this way is expensive too, but not as expensive as that last trophy hunt. Just think how nice it would be to walk in on Sunday night and tell Mama the hunt was great, that Bambi is being processed and can be picked up next week. The little woman will think you are a saint! No more "final cleaning" in the same sink your lady does the crystal in, no more dogs cruising the flower beds looking to bury a leg bone. If that isn't being a good guy, what is? Your stock on the domestic exchange may rise enough to update your collection of custom hunting gear. Certainly your golf, billiards, or quaffing skills will sharpen.

Don't, however, let any purist muddy the waters here. We've discovered this as we would a new deer trail. We've paid our dues. And just because these deer are commercially raised doesn't mean they are McGame meat. Most have been raised in the almost wilds of New Zealand and have not been force fed chocolates and champagne in some animal health spa!

Regain your position at the head of the table as you encourage your younguns to eat prime native meats. Your choice of off-site processing will soften your older daughter's opinion of your barbaric blood sports. Your hunting prowess will be telegraphed up and around the cul-de-sac, forcing your yuppie neighbors to button up about the snowmobile collection in different stages of disrepair in your driveway. You will be called "Ol' Sureshot" behind your back and there is a slight chance your property values will increase.

There are several major distributors. Have your friendly butcher call them so the meat can be delivered direct. You can order by preferred part—leg, loin, breast—and not have to force your loved ones to eat campmeats that diminish your parental authority. You can order in relatively small quantities and keep the family free of the burden of eating a monster mulie before it freezer-burns.

Orders can take a week so schedule your call accordingly. Order only slightly more than you shot last season—it's not nice to fool your loved ones and nobody likes a game hog. Always stay below the legal limit so your image as a sportsman is untarnished. Don't order three back legs. Don't take fewer dollars from the joint savings account; take more (inflation being what it is) and salt away the savings. After a couple seasons, you'll have enough set aside to take a real safari to an exotic location like Las Vegas. They have telephones there too!

Afterword:

WHY NOT HUNT DEER?

Only the really stupid deer get shot. As a deer hunter, you are part of natural selection, just what Darwin and his Southern Baptist followers have said all along. Deer hunting accidents are God's way of culling the dummies out of our ranks!

Now that you've had a chance to absorb literally centuries worth of advice, it's up to you to make it happen. Buck knows it's easier to stay at home feigning illness, death in the families, job pressures, and all kinds of deadlines. Sometimes it's cold and nasty out there. Sometimes it isn't fun at all. But it's only once a year. And only a hunter can properly pass down new traditions and old clothes.

Did Buck forget anything? Let me know. But for now, Buck stops here.

This here is Buck Peterson and woodland friends after an afternoon romp in the northern Minnesota hills. Famous game biologists from respected learning institutions can't explain Buck's success. They all say, "He's just like one of them trophy bucks themselves!"

*Other books of interest to the outdoorsperson,
from our stunning nature series.*

THE ORIGINAL ROAD KILL COOKBOOK

by B.R. "Buck" Peterson
The author of the COMPLETE GUIDE TO DEER HUNTING offers an outrageous, devastating response to the call of the open road. *Pavement Possum, Hushed Puppies,* and *Armadillo on the Half Shell* are just a few of the culinary delights which you can harvest from the "highway supermarket," using the automobile of your choice (preferably American-made). $4.95 paper, 64 pages.

FLATTENED FAUNA

by Roger Knutson
The only nature guide that millions of Americans will ever need—a guide to identifying animals once they've been flattened by dozens of vehicles and baked by the sun to an indistinct fur, scale, or feather-covered patty. Was that an old hubcap or a painted turtle? A lump of dirt or a yellow-bellied marmot? FLATTENED FAUNA provides the answers. $5.95 paper, 96 pages.

HOW TO SHIT IN THE WOODS
Second Edition, Revised

by Kathleen Meyer
"There is no easy way to say this: You have to learn how to properly defecate in the woods . . . Fortunately, former river guide Kathleen Meyer is less squeamish than the rest of us, and has written an authoritative and entertaining book."—*USA Today*.

    This revised and expanded edition of our acclaimed outdoors classic tells when and how to go when nature calls, and why it's of such vital ecological importance to do it right. $5.95 paper, 128 pages.

HOW TO HAVE SEX IN PUBLIC
WITHOUT BEING NOTICED

by Marcel Feigel
This cartoon classic is filled with novel suggestions for the adventurous outdoorsperson. $3.95 paper, 80 pages.

Available from your local bookstore, or order direct from the publisher. Please include $3.50 shipping and handling for the first book, and 50¢ for each additional book. California residents include local sales tax. Write for our free complete catalog of over 500 books and tapes.

1➔ Ten Speed Press
P. O. Box 7123
Berkeley, California 94707

For VISA, Mastercard, and American Express orders
call (800) 841-BOOK